ASPECTS OF *MACBE*

ASPECTS OF
MACBETH

ARTICLES REPRINTED FROM *SHAKESPEARE SURVEY*

EDITED BY

KENNETH MUIR

EMERITUS PROFESSOR OF ENGLISH LITERATURE
UNIVERSITY OF LIVERPOOL

AND

PHILIP EDWARDS

KING ALFRED PROFESSOR OF ENGLISH LITERATURE
UNIVERSITY OF LIVERPOOL

CAMBRIDGE UNIVERSITY PRESS

CAMBRIDGE

LONDON · NEW YORK · MELBOURNE

Published by the Syndics of the Cambridge University Press
The Pitt Building, Trumpington Street, Cambridge CB2 1RP
Bentley House, 200 Euston Road, London NW1 2DB
32 East 57th Street, New York, NY 10022, USA
296 Beaconsfield Parade, Middle Park, Melbourne 3206, Australia

Library of Congress catalogue card number: 76-56239

ISBN 0 521 21500 5 hard covers
ISBN 0 521 29176 3 paperback

This collection first published 1977
Reprinted 1978

Printed in Great Britain at the
University Press, Cambridge

CONTENTS

v

PLATES

PREFACE

These essays have been selected from the annual publication, *Shakespeare Survey*. Most of them appeared in Volume 19 (1966) which took *Macbeth* as its central theme. G. K. Hunter's essay, an assessment of the different fields of twentieth-century criticism of *Macbeth*, serves as a starting point both for the study of the play and for reading the more recent criticism of our time. Many of the essays are concerned with the material which went to the building of *Macbeth*. A well-known essay which stands its ground after a quarter of a century is Muriel Bradbrook's study of the sources, a convincing picture of the genesis of a great work of art. Glynne Wickham relates the 'hell-gate' of the porter scene to the medieval stage-tradition of the harrowing of hell. Moelwyn Merchant's essay sees Lady Macbeth in the context of demonic possession, and uses Blake to help our understanding of Hecate. Another tradition in which Lady Macbeth may be seen is the Senecan, and Inga-Stina Ewbank relates Shakespeare's heroine to the unwomanish Medea.

L. C. Knights in his famous essay *How Many Children had Lady Macbeth?* chose *Macbeth* as his battleground for his attack on the Bradley concept of character-study and insisted that Shakespeare's plays should be studied as poems. The noise of battle echoes still, and anyone who, like Kenneth Muir, further explores the rich tapestry of the play's images, has to declare his allegiances. Muir urges that a study of the imagery must support, not contradict, the understanding which 'the total experience' of the play provides. Kantak, at times taking issue with Muir, is also concerned to find the proper place within dramatic criticism for the study of the play's images. It finds poetry an aspect of character and argues this thesis from the image of the actor which reaches its summation in the 'poor player' of Macbeth's 'tomorrow' speech.

Most of these essays, therefore, suggest 'ways in' to the play, and in doing that each author suggests his own understanding and evaluation of the work. R. B. Heilman's essay begins at the centre, and scrupulously explores how it is that we can maintain that interest in the doings of a criminal hero which distinguishes the truly tragic experience from that of melodrama and morality.

K. M.
P. E.

MACBETH IN THE TWENTIETH CENTURY

BY

G. K. HUNTER

DISINTEGRATION

All editions of *Macbeth* derive from one single and authoritative text—that of the First Folio. The number of substantive emendations that modern editors see fit to introduce is quite small; and there are no passages so hopelessly corrupt that the sense is obscured. All this would argue an uncomplex task for the editor, and a simple and mercifully brief narrative for the historian of criticism. This turns out not to be the case. The discovery that the two songs (whose first lines are invoked in III, v and, again, in IV, i) exist in full texts in the manuscript of Middleton's *The Witch* has unloosed a flood of disintegration. I am more or less discounting, of course, the views of chronic disintegrators like J. M. Robertson who found (*Literary Detection*, 1931) that 'there is clear literary evidence of the past existence of a lost pre-Shakespearean *Macbeth* by Kyd'; Middleton he found to have written the Witch-scenes, the Porter-scene and the couplet tags throughout the play; there is a case for Heywood's authorship of the closing scene. IV, iii and I, ii are non-Shakespearian but unassigned. More impressive are the views of Clark and Wright, not given to rashness, who excised whole areas of the play from the Shakespeare canon, finding the bleeding sergeant in I, ii an 'absurdity', his metre 'slovenly' and his 'bombastic phraseology . . . not like Shakespeare's language even when he is most bombastic'.

The editions of Henry Cunningham (1912)—who seems really to have despised the play that was foisted upon him—of J. Q. Adams (1931) and J. Dover Wilson (1947) continue the tradition of disintegration, though with decreasing confidence and increasing elaboration of argument. Dover Wilson's argument that there were three distinct *Macbeth* texts 'during the first dozen years of the 17th century' has found few imitators; its assumptions are more elaborate than is required to account for the facts of the text; and at the merest flourish of Occam's razor it would seem to shrink away. William Empson (*Kenyon Review*, 1952) points out that what Dover Wilson sees as muddles or abridgements may be deliberate effects, part of the play's 'atmosphere':

So far from being a cut version of a tidy historical play now unfortunately lost, it is a rather massive effort, very consistently carried out, to convey the immense confusion in which those historical events actually occur.

The work of J. M. Nosworthy has struck a welcome note of sense in all this confusion. In a series of articles he found Shakespeare parallels to make the point that the last forty lines were 'Shakespearian', found that the Hecate scenes were unlike Middleton, and that the 'bombastic' speech of the bleeding sergeant was both Shakespearian and entirely appropriate to his role as a 'passionate and weighty Nuntius'—the latter point reinforced by Holger Nørgard's discovery (*The Review of English Studies*, 1955) that the sergeant echoes Daniel's *Cleopatra*, which Shakespeare read in preparation for *Antony and Cleopatra*. The 'low soliloquy of the Porter' (Clark and Wright) was at the same time moving back into favour, for reasons I discuss below (pp. 10–11). Writing in *The Library* (1947) Nosworthy made the important point that Shakespeare had woven 'all the tractable material' in Holinshed into his play, and made the important deduction that *Macbeth* had never been a long play.

This work, and the movement of the tidal waters of reintegration, left the Hecate scenes the only part of *Macbeth* that continued to be generally suspect, though occasional throwbacks, like G. B. Harrison (1951) and Lily B. Campbell (1930), continued to cast aspersions at whole areas of the play. Verity in his edition of 1901 had defended Hecate's iambic speeches on the ground that 'Shakespeare would not make the classical goddess speak in the same manner as the grim, barbaric witches'. This point was taken up and greatly elaborated by G. Wilson Knight (*The Shakespearian Tempest*, 1932), who here argues along the lines that elsewhere have enabled him to posit the authenticity of the Vision in *Cymbeline*, and the Diana scene in *Pericles*. In relation to *Macbeth* as a whole he further extends this to a general interpretation of Evil, seen both as discordant with good (the Witches) and as completely at harmony with itself (Hecate); common-sense clearly will have greater difficulty in accepting this part of the argument. The other most vocal defender of the Hecate scenes is Richard Flatter (*Shakespeare Jahrbuch*, 1957), who else-where (*Shakespeare's Producing Hand*, 1948) seeks to defend Folio lineation as deliberately contrived theatrical effect. Between 1958 and 1960 Flatter and J. P. Cutts carried on a somewhat iterative and indecisive argument about the stage-directions in the Hecate scenes, in the pages of *Shake-speare Jahrbuch*.

The defenders of Hecate are, however, the exceptions; general opinion (represented *inter alia* by the editions of Kittredge (1939), Kenneth Muir (1951) and Eugene Waith (1954)) leans against authenticity; but the shaky ground on which the whole argument is conducted may be seen from Lily B. Campbell's assumption (*Shakespeare's Tragic Heroes*, 1930) that III, v must be non-Shakespearian, for the very reason that proves its Shakespearian quality to Flatter—its preparative function, in anticipation of IV, i.

A sensible middle opinion is represented (once again) by Nosworthy, who (*The Review of English Studies*, 1948) accepts the songs as Middleton's; and thinks that the Hecate speeches were written to introduce and justify the appearance of that lady in the songs. He does not exclude the possibility that they may have been written by Shakespeare.

TOPICAL REFERENCE

The connexion of this play with King James I has long been asserted. Capell could say (in 1779) that it was 'acknowledged on all hands'. Malone suggested that *Macbeth* might have been 'first exhibited' when King Christian IV of Denmark was visiting London (17 July–11 August 1606). These points have been taken up generally (e.g. by J. Q. Adams in his edition of 1931) and vastly expanded in the most important recent study—*The Royal Play of 'Macbeth'*, by H. N. Paul (1950). Paul adds some interesting new points to the argument that the play was written for the two kings. He notes that the second battle in Holinshed was fought against 'the Danes', and that Shakespeare alters this to 'the Norweyans'—as befits a courtier addressing the Scottish and Danish monarchs. He suggests that the 'milk of concord' line (IV, iii, 98) refers to the arch of welcome which greeted James and Christian on 31 July 1606. Elsewhere he greatly amplifies existing references, as where he traces James's changing taste in demonology, or his changing attitude to 'touching' for scrofula.

It must be added, however, that Paul exhibits more industry than discrimination. His notion of the play as an aesthetic organism is less effective than his sense of it as a compliment. Many of his arguments—such as the one that Macbeth is a conjurer in IV, iii—are both curious and unproductive. His use of details of poetic or theatrical technique is nearly always distorted by his desire to multiply topical references. The Appendix to Kenneth Muir's new Arden edition (ninth edition, 1962) provides a convenient short survey of principal points from Paul's book.

The references in *Macbeth* to 'equivocation' and to the Gunpowder plot have, likewise, a long history of comment; but their interest has been strengthened by some recent investigations. In *I, William Shakespeare* (1937) Leslie Hotson traces connexions between Shakespeare's known friends and men involved in the plot. H. L. Rogers (*Double Profit in 'Macbeth'*, 1964) sees the whole play riddled with references to equivocation and duplicity. In *Publications of the Modern Language Association* (1964) Frank L. Huntley discusses '*Macbeth* and the background of Jesuitical equivocation' and shows the extent to which the mode of the witches' prophecies echoes the Jesuit doctrine, substituting Satan for God.

SOURCES

No principal source of *Macbeth* has been found to replace Holinshed's *Chronicles*. H. N. Paul has picked up many supplementary suggestions that have attached themselves to the play—that Shakespeare had read Buchanan's Latin history of Scotland, Leslie's *De... Rebus Gestis Scotorum* and Skene's *Scots Acts*. Dover Wilson (1947) has repeated Mrs Stopes's suggestion (1916) that Shakespeare drew on William Stewart's *Chronicles of Scotland*. It may well be that Shakespeare had read one or all of these, but, if so, they do not seem to have influenced him into any piece of writing that was impossible to a creative use of Holinshed. Dr Gwinn's *Tres Sybillae*, who greeted James I when he went to Oxford in 1605, are more interesting; but have been known since the eighteenth century. The debates at Oxford on the questions 'whether imagination is able to produce real effects' and 'whether the child acquires characteristics from his nurse's milk', also cited by Paul, throw interesting sidelights on the kind of thinking that the seventeenth century brought to bear on such subjects. Lily B. Campbell (*Shakespeare Quarterly*, 1951), like Paul, and like Jane H. Jack (*ELH*, 1955), thinks of James I's *Basilicon Doron* as a source-book for the play; indeed she prefers to think that James's writings are the source of that passage in IV, 3, in which Malcolm denies the princely virtues, which Paul had referred to the arch of triumph welcoming James and Christian into London. Kenneth Muir in *Shakespeare's Sources* (1957) notices, in addition to matters already discussed, an apparent echo of Daniel's *The Queen's Arcadia*. He also discusses debts to Seneca and to the Bible, some of which have been known for a long time. The Biblical echoes are, of course, discussed at large in Richmond Noble's *Shakespeare's Biblical Knowledge* (1935).

In an article (page 12 of this volume) that is unusually thoughtful for a source-study Muriel C. Bradbrook makes the point that the political 'sources' of *Macbeth* are in the end less important than an analogue like *Lucrece* which traces the 'inner structure' of the play from violence to self-destruction.

Those who survey the history of witch-definition in *Macbeth* are liable to find the identity of these ladies as equivocal as their prophecies. The very source, indeed, supplied Shakespeare with two contradictory definitions, speaking of 'three women in strange and wild apparel, resembling creatures of elder world ... these women were either the weird sisters, that is (as ye would say) the goddesses of destiny or else some nymphs or fairies, endued with knowledge of prophecy by their necromantical science'.

Bradley, holding that 'character in action' is the stuff of Shakespearian tragedy, was not willing to admit that the witches were more than clairvoyant: 'There is not a syllable in *Macbeth* to imply that they are anything but women.' He sees that the power of the protagonist is fatally infringed if he cannot choose his own destiny and therefore asserts that 'the prophecies of the Witches are presented simply as dangerous circumstances with which Macbeth has to deal ... Macbeth is, in the ordinary sense, perfectly free in regard to them.' Shakespeare took over, in Bradley's view, the descriptions of witch-superstitions which he found in Reginald Scot, and used them to operate upon the minds of his audience, to provide convenient symbols for the evil tendencies in the world at large. Shakespeare took nothing from Holinshed except the name 'Weird Sisters'—'which certainly no more suggested to a London audience the Parcae of one mythology or the Norns of another than it does today'.

The Norns had been suggested by Fleay (1876) and by Miss Charlotte Carmichael (1879); later the suggestion was lent greater authority, when it was adopted by Kittredge (1939). Kittredge, without Bradley's interest in avoiding even the suggestion of fatalism, baldly supposes that Shakespeare must have meant what Holinshed meant by 'Weird Sisters': 'they not only foresaw the future, but decreed it.... Thus the tragedy of *Macbeth* is inevitably fatalistic, but Shakespeare attempts no solution of the problem of free-will and predestination. . . . He never gives us the impression that a man is not responsible for his own acts.'

Walter Clyde Curry, in *Shakespeare's Philosophical Patterns* (1937), investigates, with great assiduity and learning, the whole 'metaphysic of evil' that appears in *Macbeth*. Starting from the definition of 'nature's germens' (IV, i, 58)—in the scholastic thought which he supposes Shakespeare to have 'more or less unconsciously assimilated'—he finds that the witches 'are not ordinary witches ... are demons or devils in the form of witches'. The witch-attributes he takes to be 'popular domestic symbols'; but the philosophical reality is 'the metaphysical world of evil intelligences [but] distilled by Shakespeare's imagination and concentrated in those marvellous dramatic symbols, the Weird Sisters'. Curry's demonic forces can 'animate nature and ensnare human souls by means of diabolical persuasion, by hallucination, infernal illusion and possession'. They cannot plant thoughts in the mind. But they may 'incite to thought' and kindle desires. They cannot know what *must* happen, but have a contingent knowledge of the future. And they wait everywhere to disturb and torment human weakness.

H. N. Paul, *The Royal Play of 'Macbeth'* (1950), thinks that the witches are not simply witches, but (more precisely) 'Scotch witches', i.e. witches as described in the *Demonology* of James I, and found in action in Holinshed's account of King Duff and the witches of Forres, working under the control of the devil.

Another view of Shakespeare's attitude to the double definition of the witches in Holinshed appears in Willard Farnham, *Shakespeare's Tragic Frontier* (1950). Farnham quotes very extensively from the literature of this period to show how far 'fairy', 'elf', 'hag' and 'witch' were interchangeable terms. For example Peter Heylyn's 1625 account of the Macbeth story speaks of 'Fairies, or Witches (Weirds the Scots call them)'. Farnham's final suggestion is that Shakespeare used the words of Holinshed's first definition, i.e. 'Weird Sisters', but interpreted them in the light of his alternative definition, as 'nymphs or fairies', able to see the future, but not to control it.

The difficulty of the witches for a modern audience is an old subject of discussion. A. P. Rossiter gives it a new and more authentically theatrical twist by suggesting (*Angel with Horns*, 1961) that only masks as *vile* as those of some African devils would serve today to make the point required. J. R. Brown, *Shakespeare: The Tragedy of Macbeth* (1963), quotes Ingmar Bergman on the same theatrical difficulty.

INTERPRETATION

Macbeth has long been considered one of Shakespeare's 'most sublime' plays, if only because of the obvious analogues between it and Greek tragedies—see 'Shakespeare's *Macbeth* arranged as an ancient tragedy' in R. G. Moulton's *Ancient Classical Drama* (1890). But in this century it has probably attracted fewer enthusiasts than the other 'great' tragedies in Bradley. John Bailey, *Shakespeare* (1929), finds that 'it neither interests the mind nor moves the heart, nor fills the imagination, as do *Hamlet* and *Othello* and *Lear*'; G. B. Harrison (*Shakespeare's Tragedies*, 1951) thinks that '*Macbeth* has been extravagantly over-praised. It is the weakest of Shakespeare's great tragedies, and so full of blemishes that it is hard to believe that one man wrote it.' On the other hand those who have preferred 'poetry' to 'drama' (supposing these to be separable) have continued to be attracted by its intensity. Of the Bradleian 'great' tragedies, *Macbeth* is probably the one which is least centred on reactions to quasi-real characters; Johnson's comment is worth remembering here: 'It has no nice discrimination of character; the events are too great to admit the influence of particular dispositions, and the course of the action necessarily determines the conduct of the agents.' It is no accident that F. R. Leavis's anti-Bradleian spoof question 'How many children had Lady Macbeth?' was referred to this particular play.

In fairness to Bradley it has to be pointed out, however, that some of the finest statements of the indeterminacy of 'character' in a poetic structure appear in the *Macbeth* essays in *Shakespearean Tragedy*. Macbeth and Lady Macbeth, he tells us, 'are never detached in imagination from the atmosphere which surrounds them and adds to their grandeur and terror. It is, as it were, continued into their souls. For within them is all that we felt without—the darkness of night, lit with the flame of tempest and the hues of blood, and haunted by wild and direful shapes.' Bradley's evocation of the poetic atmosphere of Macbeth is justly celebrated as a *locus classicus*:

Images like those of the babe torn smiling from the breast and dashed to death; of pouring the sweet milk of concord into hell; of the earth shaking in fever; of the frame of things disjointed; of sorrows striking heaven on the face, so that it resounds and yells out like syllables of dolour; of the mind lying in restless ecstasy on a rack; of the mind full of scorpions; of the tale told by an idiot, full of sound and fury;—all keep the imagination moving on a 'wild and violent sea' while it is scarcely for a moment permitted to dwell on thoughts of peace and beauty. In its language, as in its action, the drama is full of tumult and storm.

Bradley had not, of course, developed the study of themes and images in the systematic way of Miss Spurgeon and her successors; and it may be thought that it is in such works that *Macbeth* has come into its own. In *Shakespeare's Imagery* (1935) *Macbeth* occupies more space than any other single play. Miss Spurgeon sees it as 'more rich and varied, more highly imaginative, more unapproachable by any other writer than any other single play . . . the ideas in the imagery are in themselves more imaginative, more subtle and complex than in other plays'. She pays special attention to trains of images concerned with clothing, with light and dark, with reverberation, with disease and with horse-riding.

Cleanth Brooks also chooses this play, in his celebrated essay, 'The Naked Babe and the Cloak of Manliness' (*The Well Wrought Urn*, 1947), to make the general point that images that may seem pointlessly grotesque in isolation turn out to be structurally important when pursued throughout a play. Starting from the celebrated image of the chamberlains' daggers 'unmannerly breeched with gore' he shows how this may be justified in terms of the importance of disguise throughout the play. In a critical atmosphere which rated irony and paradox as the highest virtues *Macbeth* was unlikely to be an underrated play. H. L. Gardner has, however—in *The Business of Criticism* (1959)—pointed out a tendency in Cleanth Brooks's essay to substitute patterns for the genuine 'Shakespearian depth of human feeling' in the individual passage; and perhaps this is inseparable from sustained image-study.

Other themes have been pursued by other authors. Few image-hunters seem to have followed the counter-stroke of Wolfgang Clemen who, in *The Development of Shakespeare's Imagery* (1951), excluded *Macbeth* from his image-study of the tragedies. John Lawlor (*Shakespeare Quarterly*, 1957) sees the idea of Macbeth as an actor 'alone against a potentially dangerous world of observers' as central. The imagery of time in the play is eloquently explored by Stephen Spender (*Penguin New Writing*, 1941)—a point on which, however, he had been anticipated by J. M. Murry, *Shakespeare* (1936).

Another theme—that of manhood—is taken up by Eugene Waith in *ELH* (1950): Lady Macbeth's power over her husband depends on persuading him to accept a partial and improper definition of manliness. As Waith says, 'the soldier may avoid the danger of effeminacy only to incur the still greater danger of brutishness'.

Brents Stirling, on the other hand, sees the play as unified round the themes of 'raptness' ('look how our partner's rapt') and inverted nature (*Unity in Shakespearian Tragedy*, 1956). Francis Fergusson (*The Human Image in Dramatic Literature*, 1957) takes the phrase 'outrun the pauser reason' to be the key to the thematic structure.

It has indeed become something of a cliché of modern criticism to say that the essential structure of *Macbeth* is 'to be sought in the poetry' (L. C. Knights), that the characters 'are not shaped primarily to conform to a psychological verisimilitude, but to make explicit the intellectual statements with which the play is concerned' (Irving Ribner), that Lady Macbeth, Macbeth and Banquo 'are parts of a pattern, a design; are images or symbols' (A. P. Rossiter). The packed and economical structure of the play (often noticed) and the relative absence of episodes of detached realistic observation (like those of the players or the gravediggers in *Hamlet*) have made *Macbeth* seem particularly suitable for symbolic (or dogmatic) interpretations, and expositions of this kind have not been lacking. A great many of the subsequent lines of such interpretation appeared first in G. Wilson Knight's essay 'The Milk of Concord' in *The Imperial Theme*

(1931), a more complete, more coherent and (I think) a more influential treatment than that in *The Wheel of Fire* (1930). 'The Milk of Concord' presents a structure tensed between 'life-themes' and 'death-themes'; attention is directed to the failure of such 'natural' activities as sleeping and eating. The broken feasts of Act I and Act III find their answer in the witches' banquet of Act IV. Time is disordered; the future is compromised and the *natural* processes of childhood and development are cut off. The perception that the play is 'about' Nature and unnaturalness has been developed more sensitively (but also more moralistically) by L. C. Knights (*Some Shakespearean Themes*, 1959). Nature offers man a choice between creativeness and destructiveness. We respond to the choice because it is embodied in the poetic texture of the play.

Symbolic interpretation of a Shakespearian play which is full of Biblical phrases and images is bound to become explicitly Christian sooner or later, and there is quite a body of modern criticism which has explicitly Christian designs on *Macbeth*. Roy Walker, *The Time is Free* (n.d. (1949)), is less critically hamstrung by this intention than one might have supposed he would be. Excesses of interpretation, such as finding Seyton equivalent to Satan, equating Hecate with 'Lady Macbeth's guilty spirit', or treating Macbeth's pursuit of 'the son' (Malcolm, Donalbain, Fleance, young Macduff) as an analogy of anti-Christ—these are not central to the book. Acute perceptions abound (some anticipated by Wilson Knight); one may cite his antithetical placing of the two women in the play (p. 153).

The same general point may be made about J. A. Bryant, Jr (*Hippolyta's View*, 1961). Bryant's central critical point is that Macbeth's two great qualities, loyalty and bravery, are released from their double harness by the witches' prophecy, and, pulling against one another, pull Macbeth apart. This is not necessarily a Christian interpretation, though in Bryant's handling it becomes one, and one can enjoy its incidental acutenesses without accepting the whole framework in which they appear.

The other complete volume devoted to christianizing *Macbeth*—G. R. Elliott's *Dramatic Providence in Macbeth* (1958)—is, unfortunately, without acuteness. Elliott's book is much more tied to character-response than either Walker's or Bryant's; he asks us to identify with a sinful soul set in a theological framework. We are supposed always to be on the edges of our seats watching for signs of grace or repentance. Thus, speaking of 'Wake Duncan with thy knocking . . .', etc., at the end of II, ii, he says 'Will Macbeth's deepening remorse open the way for true humility and repentance? That major question overshadows the minor one: will his guilt be discovered by his peers?' (p. 90). One feels that Mr Elliott would have profited greatly by reading H. L. Gardner's 'Milton's "Satan" and the Theme of Damnation in Elizabethan Tragedy' (*Essays and Studies of the English Association*, 1948), where the dangers of simple-minded christianizing are spelled out with lucid perceptiveness.

Analogous to the Christian view of the play is that approach which looks upon it as a myth or ritual, but without specific meaning. Thus John Holloway, *The Story of the Night* (1961), finds Macbeth (like other tragic heroes) to be 'a scapegoat, a lord of misrule who has turned life into riot for his limited time, and is then driven out and destroyed by the forces which embody the fertile vitality and the communal happiness of the social group'.

H. C. Goddard, *The Meaning of Shakespeare* (1951), sees the play as a winter–spring ritual, in which the spring maiden overcomes the winter king. Both these authors make much of May-game analogies to Malcolm's army advancing on Dunsinane with green boughs held over their heads—presumably the clearest 'anthropological' moment in the play.

Yet another way of looking at the play, without putting response to individual characters at the centre, is to call it a morality play, and this has been done by several authors; but it is not clear that this nomenclature can take us very far, critically. A. E. Hunter, writing in *Shakespeare Association Bulletin* for 1937, was probably the first to devote much space to '*Macbeth* as a Morality'. The most useful element in the morality analogue would seem to be that which concerns 'flat' characterization—a feature of *Macbeth* that had drawn discriminating praise from Quiller-Couch (*Shakespeare's Workmanship*, 1918). F. P. Wilson (*Elizabethan and Jacobean*, 1945) notes that: 'In *Macbeth* many characters are brought in with no attempt to make them individual: the sergeant, the messenger, the doctor, the waiting-woman, the murderers, the "Old Man" and we may add Ross, Angus and Lennox . . . are without personality as much as the characters in a morality-play.'

IV, iii is one scene in the play which has been particularly affected by this modern tendency to take 'flatness' as description rather than evaluation. Traditionally, this has been considered the least successful scene in the play, close to Holinshed only because Shakespeare was not interested enough to create new material. Grierson in his edition of 1914 calls it 'a perfunctory paraphrase from Holinshed'. To many critics interested in theme, however, the scene appears to be brilliantly successful, a keystone of the structure. Francis Fergusson sees it as the *peripeteia*, the point at which the tide turns effectively against Macbeth, in which the isolation of his victims is overcome by Grace and by suffering. The thematic significance of *testing* our friends, of the 'good' King Edward, and of 'the Evil' that he cures, are points regularly made in this context.

The flatness of the individual characters who make up the opposition to Macbeth is sometimes thought to mark a weakness in the play. Mark Van Doren (*Shakespeare*, 1941) finds that '*Macbeth* is not in the fullest sense a tragedy' and William Rosen (*Shakespeare and the Craft of Tragedy*, 1960), taking up the same point, compares the simple optimism at the end of *Macbeth* with the intense questioning generated at the end of *Lear*, to the discredit (of course) of the former.

From another point of view, the simplicity of the end of *Macbeth* is a mark of its relation to the history plays. The relationship between the Christian view and the historical view is the subject of an article by Jane H. Jack (*ELH*, 1955). Mrs Jack shows how James I's political interests were coloured at every turn by his conviction that the Kingdom of Satan was everywhere around him. *Macbeth* echoes the obsessions of James (and the age), finding its Christian focus in the Old Testament (Saul and the Witch of Endor) and in the Apocalypse, rather than in the Gospels. Tyranny is represented as a spiritual condition rather than a political problem. The historical action of the play becomes 'an imaginative exploration of evil in Biblical terms'.

W. A. Armstrong (*The Review of English Studies*, 1946) sees the play in terms of a recurrent 'dramatic convention' which sets the lawful and hereditary king (Duncan, Edward, Malcolm) against the criminal and usurping tyrant. Hardin Craig (1948) classes *Macbeth* (along with *Antony and Cleopatra* and *Coriolanus*) as a 'Great Political Play'. The most successful treatment of *Macbeth* along these lines is probably that of E. M. W. Tillyard, *Shakespeare's History Plays* (1944). Tillyard sees *Macbeth* as the 'culminating version' of Shakespeare's concern with the man of action '. . . the finest of all mirrors for magistrates'. The relationship of 'flat' characterization to this focus is quite obvious from his comment on Malcolm: '[Malcolm] is the ideal

8

ruler who has subordinated all his personal pleasures, and with them all personal charm, to his political obligations.'

Jan Kott (*Shakespeare, Our Contemporary*, 1964) follows in this line of describing the play as a history play, but distinguishes between the 'grand mechanism' of Shakespeare's 'histories' (which operates *upon* individuals), and the existentialist responsibility of the individual hero in *Macbeth*.

All this concern for the *pattern* of Macbeth has diverted interest from the hero as a man. None the less the reaction (even of critics) to stage-figures as if to real people is not finally repressible, and few treatments succeed in ignoring the hero altogether. But the modern treatments of Macbeth the man have responded to the general distrust of individualism and have drifted in a generally reductive and anti-heroic direction. Of course, there are exceptions. Bradley's 'He never forfeits our sympathy' has been echoed most enthusiastically by John Masefield in his Home University Library *Shakespeare* (n.d. (1911)); and H. B. Charlton (1948) and Peter Alexander (1939) are generally sympathetic. But most critics, for one reason or another, have seemed anxious to de-sentimentalize Macbeth. The prevalence of clothing imagery with its presentation of Macbeth as a dwarfish thief was thought by Miss Spurgeon to provide a counterweight to the romantic image of a heroic Macbeth. From very different premises, Schücking (*Character Problems*, 1922) saw him as a self-regarding, essentially ignoble character, more hindered by nerves than by conscience. Lily B. Campbell (1930) presents him as oscillating between fear and rashness, one who 'begins with the courage that is not real courage and ends with the courage that is not real courage'. A. P. Rossiter thinks of Macbeth's intellect as 'quite the most normal—even commonplace—among Shakespeare's gallery of minds'. Stoll (*Review of English Studies*, 1943; *From Shakespeare to Joyce*, 1944) and Schücking (*The Baroque Character of the Elizabethan Tragic Hero*, 1938) have, of course, their own drastic ways of resolving the tension between Macbeth's heroic nature and his crimes: they divide the character into two irreconcilable elements, yoked together only by theatrical legerdemain. J. I. M. Stewart (*Character and Motive in Shakespeare*, 1949) asserts, against this, the psychological plausibility of such tensions: 'Before *Macbeth* we ought not to abandon the conception of a "psychology" (as Mr Stoll would have us do) but deepen it.'

Much nineteenth-century admiration for *Macbeth* had stemmed from the quality of his imagination. Bradley summed up a great deal of this when he said that his imagination was 'the best part of him' and that 'if he had obeyed it he would have been safe'. An article by C. C. Clarke (*Durham University Journal*, 1960) attacks these assumptions and does something to restore to Macbeth his status as the actor as well as the principal witness of his crimes; Macbeth is not simply the victim of his imagination; 'he is also, and more simply, a man who fails to think clearly on a moral issue'. A useful additional caveat has also been entered by W. Rosen (1960): 'Shakespeare purposely elevates Macbeth's stature above that of Duncan and Banquo. Too often this is not stressed . . . in studies which offer patterns of order against those of disorder.' These may be signs that the individuality of Macbeth is beginning to emerge from the sea of images in which it has so long lain submerged.

The Bradleian method was, inevitably, much weaker with minor characters than with major. His treatment of Banquo is an obvious case. In Bradley's view, Banquo began as a foil to Macbeth, but soon lost this role. His soliloquy in III, i ('Thou hast it now—King, Cawdor, Glamis, all . . . ') was taken to show that he had failed culpably to make his suspicions of Macbeth known abroad. When it emerges in the same scene that Banquo is now the king's chief counsellor, Bradley cannot resist the suspicion that he has been bribed into silence. It is interesting to note that George Wilson Knight, starting from a very different point, finds the same 'bond of evil between Banquo and Macbeth'. But most modern critics are anxious to keep Macbeth and Banquo as distinct as possible, taking forward to its logical conclusion Bradley's perception that the characters of the play fit into its atmosphere as parts into a structure. S. Nagarajan (*Shakespeare Quarterly*, 1956) sees the two men as 'placed' by the play in polarities of good and evil that 'characterization' cannot be allowed to infringe. Leo Kirschbaum (*Essays in Criticism*, 1957) notes that Banquo is not a whole man but 'a dramaturgic foil to Macbeth'. He points to a pattern of image contrasts between Lady Macbeth and Banquo which serve to place these characters at opposite sides of the wavering and central protagonist.

The movement that has changed Banquo from a person to a 'dramaturgic foil' has also affected Lady Macbeth. The relationship between the two criminals is very liable to sentimentalism, of the kind of Moulton's 'wife-like, she has no sphere but the career of her husband' or 'she has had the feminine lot of being shut out from active life and her genius and energy have been turned inwards'. Moulton's treatment is based (like that of many modern critics) on a perception that the Macbeths are *complementary* creations; but modern critics tend to see them as complementary in terms of pattern and idea rather than in terms of personality. Maynard Mack's 'The Jacobean Shakespeare' (*Jacobean Theatre*, 1960), for example, makes the point that the heroic tone of voice needs a foil, if it is to be acceptable. So Lady Macbeth has the same function as Horatio, urging upon the hero's metaphysical anguish the 'common-sense' of 'consider it not so curiously'. Mack again relates the sleepwalking scene to the total dramatic pattern rather than to the individual psychology of Lady Macbeth.

Macbeth is absent at this juncture . . . has not in fact been visible during two long scenes and will not be visible again till the next scene after this. In the interval, the slaying at Macduff's castle and the conversations between Malcolm and Macduff keep him before us in his capacity as tyrant, murderer, 'Hell-kite', seen from the outside. But Lady Macbeth's sleep-walking is, I think, Shakespeare's device for keeping him before us in his capacity as tragic hero and sufferer. . . . The 'slumbery agitation', the 'thick-coming fancies That keep her from her rest': these by a kind of poetical displacement, we may apply to him as well as to her. . . . We are, of course, conscious as we watch the scene, that this is Lady Macbeth suffering the metaphysical aspects of murder that she did not believe in; we may also be conscious that the remorse pictured here tends to distinguish her from her husband, who for some time has been giving his 'initiate fear' the 'hard use' he said it lacked, with dehumanizing consequences. Yet in some way the pity of this situation suffuses him as well as her, the more so because in every word she utters his presence beside her is supposed. . . . Such speeches as this . . . we might call umbrella speeches, since more than one consciousness may shelter under them.

The developing perception that *Macbeth* is not so much the story of an evil deed and its consequences, but rather an exploration of the meaning of Evil and its ramifications—this, more than any textual revolution, has freed a number of scenes from the suspicion of bastardy. A taste for irony and paradox, for the baroque clash of opposites—especially evident in what S. L.

Bethell called 'The Popular Tradition'—has been effective in making the Porter's speeches a centre for appreciative comment. Kenneth Muir devotes a substantial section of his Arden Introduction to this scene, defending it on grounds of (a) theatrical necessity; (b) intensification of horror; (c) thematic continuity; (d) stylistic continuity; (e) to 'cut the cable that moored his tragedy to a particular spot in space and time'.

J. Harcourt (*Shakespeare Quarterly*, 1961) concentrates on the symbolic content of the Porter's imagination and of his whole situation as 'Porter of Hell-gate'. The analogy of the Infernal Porter in the medieval 'Harrowing of Hell' plays is closer than is usually noted. Christ comes to hell in these plays and awakens hell and its porter with his thunderous command, *Attollite portas*, etc. Macduff is the Christ-figure who hammers at the door of Macbeth's hell, and he is well suited for the role. His subsequent career carries forward the analogy. As Christ enters and defeats the devil, so Macduff defeats Macbeth, emerges at the end of the play with his enemy's head on a pole and declares that 'the time is free'.

William Blissett (*Shakespeare Quarterly*, 1959) sees an analogy between the Porter's view of drunken lechery and Macbeth's political ambition, provoked in desire by the methods he adopts, but taken down in performance.

On the other hand, Terence Hawkes, *Shakespeare and the Reason* (1964), sees the porter's remarks on lechery as paralleling those of Lady Macbeth on manliness. Murder bears the same relation to politics as lechery does to love.

An interesting historical note by J. W. Spargo in *Adams Memorial Studies* (1948) helps to integrate the knocking on the door with the other death-portents in the scene of the murder— the owl's cry and the wolf's howl. In time of plague the 'knocking at the gate' signified the search for dead bodies; and the noise on the Globe stage must have reinforced the sense of a moral plague in the castle by carrying its original audience's minds back to the terror and the horror of their own plague visitations.

© G. K. HUNTER 1966

THE SOURCES OF *MACBETH*

BY

M. C. BRADBROOK

A very broad definition of 'sources' must be my excuse for considering so familiar a topic as the origins of *Macbeth*. In this, the most concentrated of the tragedies, a particularly wide diversity of material was fused into unity. "In the quick forge and working-house of thought", Shakespeare wrought at white heat. The material to be considered falls into three classes. First, the Scottish and English Chronicles supplied the facts, and one important scene; secondly, various works on witchcraft and demonology, including those of King James, gave some material for the witches' scenes (but here the interest lies rather in Shakespeare's innovations than in his borrowings); thirdly, earlier works by Shakespeare himself present in a simpler form some of the ingredients of this play, and an examination of what might be called the internal sources elucidates its inward structure. The repetitions, echoes and restatements which are to be detected in Shakespeare offer more than mere opportunity for pedantic correlation; they are alternative statements, varied embodiments of those deep-seated and permanent impulses which underlie all his work and make it, in spite of its variety, a vast and comprehensive whole—a single structure, though of Gothic design.

In reading through Holinshed's voluminous Scottish Chronicles, Shakespeare would come, about a third of the way through, upon the story of Duncan, the eighty-fourth king according to that account, and the narrative with which we are all familiar. The chronicle gives a brief and bald summary of reign after reign, describing the same round of violence, murder, rebellion and general turbulence. It is as monotonous as the series of apocryphal portraits of these early kings to be seen in Holyrood Palace; and the power of its monotony is considerable. The picture of a strange, bleak, haunted world emerges, where savage beings fulfil the passionate cycle of their dreadful lives as if under enchanted compulsion.[1] But why, in reading through these legendary stories, did Shakespeare stop where he did?

The story of Duncan and Macbeth glorified the ancestors of King James, both the ancient house of Macalpine, and in Banquo, an imaginary figure invented by Hector Boece during the fifteenth century, the later Stewart line. It also introduced the weird sisters, whose prophecies might be adapted to foretell the happy future rule of King James himself, and who were at the same time akin to the North Berwick witches whose practices against him had provided one of the most celebrated witch-trials of the age. Moreover, Malcolm Canmore, husband of the English princess Margaret and initiator of many new customs, stood at the beginning of one new age in Scottish history, as James, heir to the united crowns of Scotland and England, stood at the beginning of another. A royal command performance was clearly in view from the very inception of the play.

In the Chronicle, the history of Macbeth is briefly told, but Shakespeare shaped it both by expansion and compression. He crammed into a single act of war the rebellion of Macdonwald, two Danish invasions and the revolt of Cawdor—which happened only *after* the prophecy in Holinshed. The whole account of how Duncan was murdered he took from elsewhere, the

12

murder of King Duff; though Macbeth's stratagem to send into the Danish camp supplies of drugged food and surprise them "so amazed that they were unable to make any defence" might have suggested the drugging of the grooms. In the Chronicle, Macbeth slew Duncan in open revolt, and no indications of remorse are given either before or after the event. The long reign of Macbeth Shakespeare shortens into a few weeks; the wizard who prophesied to Macbeth about Birnam Wood merges with the weird sisters; Macbeth's death takes place before Dunsinane, and not at the end of an inglorious flight. In sum, the debt to the Chronicle is of the slightest; so bald a narrative gave Shakespeare the merest skeleton of a plot. There is, however, one scene, that between Malcolm and Macduff in England, which is reported in very great detail. Indeed, it is out of all focus in the Chronicle and occupies almost as much space as the whole of the rest of the reign. This scene represents Shakespeare's greatest debt to Holinshed; clearly it took his eye, and here perhaps is the germ of how he first conceived the play.

Malcolm's self-accusations are much more convincing to the present age than they were to the nineteenth century, when this scene was generally disliked. It was usual to cut it for stage performance. Yet an exile trying to evade the trap of his totalitarian enemy might plausibly test the reactions of his promised supporters. In a world still full of displaced persons and *agents provocateurs*, this scene can be harrowing. In Holinshed, the whole incident is weakened by the fact that both Malcolm and Macduff know of the murder of Macduff's family before the dialogue begins, so that it is hardly conceivable that Macduff could at this time be Macbeth's agent. Shakespeare, on the other hand, makes his leaving of the defenceless 'wife and child' a reasonable cause of suspicion to the young prince. Macduff does not answer Malcolm's query on this point. It is the silence of a man embittered and mature, deeply mortified by such incomprehension of the depths of sacrifice for which his loyalty prepared him.

Here again the modern reader may add his personal endorsement. In 1942 I had the honour to meet in London one of the highest officers of the French Navy, who had escaped from France after the German occupation to fight from this country. He too left his wife and child exposed to the retaliation of the enemy. In those days no one asked him why.

In Holinshed, Malcolm accuses himself of licentiousness, avarice and promise-breaking, and it is only the last which drives Macduff to renounce him. Promise-keeping is so essential to the ruler that although as all treatises on government declared—and particularly King James's[2]—it is the bounden duty of the subject to conceal the ill deeds of rulers and not even to let his *thoughts* harbour any treasonable reproof of them, yet this particular crime is indefensible. Holinshed makes the rather subtle point that while Malcolm is diffident about his other crimes, he seems to expect Macduff to conceal the last. Shakespeare omits the irony, but he was engaged in adding to the list of crimes, mentioning especially contentiousness, which, as Dover Wilson points out,[3] would be particularly obnoxious to the pacifist James. Malcolm's final speech constitutes almost a definition by contraries of the perfect ruler.

Such ingenious dissimulation would appear to the royal auditor a proof of his wisdom, more striking that it was precocious—and the more likely to foreshadow that of his illustrious descendant. Might not James also remember those ten painful months following the Ruthven Raid in 1582, when as a boy of eighteen he had to practise dissimulation with the gang who kidnapped him and forced him to govern in accordance with their faction? "Better bairns greet nor bearded men", exclaimed Lord Ruthven, when James at his first capture burst into tears.

13

The King never forgot, and years later he contrived Lord Ruthven's death should pay for it. Such memories might well have recurred and given to the scene of Malcolm's exile a deep personal significance.

The ruler was always allowed to practise extraordinary stratagems in view of his extra responsibilities, as the Duke of Vienna did in *Measure for Measure*. Malcolm was showing himself fit to rule—cleverer than his father, who knew no art to find the mind's construction in the face, and did not probe below a fair appearance.

In his recent book on Shakespeare,[4] Hardin Craig has classed *Macbeth* among the political tragedies, and there is no doubt that it was more than a personal tragedy which happened to be about princes. The natures of an ill-governed and a well-governed kingdom are contrasted throughout the latter half of the play. Here Shakespeare moved away from the Chronicle, and relied partly on other works, including those of King James, and partly on those views which had formed in his own mind during the writing of his English histories.

The relation between the King and the body politic is a sympathetic one. When the King is sick or disordered, the land is disordered too. First we are given the picture of a happy kingdom, in which Duncan and his thanes support and respect each other. Duncan plants honours, and labours to make them full of growing. His subjects return to him all the bounties with which he nourishes them, in duty and service. In her welcome Lady Macbeth falsely strikes this note of devotion, which Duncan repays with an old man's gallant politeness.

After his coronation, Macbeth tries vainly at his feast to recreate the atmosphere of close-knit amity. But "honour, love, obedience, troops of friends" he must not look to have. His thanes look forward to the time when they may "do faithful homage, and receive free honours", but the Scotland they inhabit is disordered, sick, a distracted body swollen with evil humours. This picture of the distracted kingdom is familiar from the plays of *Richard II, Henry IV* and *Richard III*, where it is described at more length. Even Macbeth sees that his land is diseased (v, iii). He himself is haunted with the sleeplessness that tormented the usurper Bolingbroke, and to read the opening of the third act of *Henry IV Part II* is like listening to an overture to *Macbeth*:

> O sleep, O gentle sleep,
> Nature's soft nurse, how have I frighted thee,
> That thou no more wilt weigh my eye-lids down,
> And steep my senses in forgetfulness?...
> Then you perceive the body of our kingdom,
> How foul it is; what rank diseases grow,
> And with what danger, near the heart of it?   (III, i, 6–9, 38–40)

Malcolm is "the medicine of the sickly weal", the 'sovereign flower' who comes with the blessing and aid of the saintly Edward. The reference in IV, i to the Confessor's sacred powers of healing was an especial compliment to James who prided himself on the inherited gift of 'the healing benediction'; but it was also necessary as a counterweight to the picture of Macbeth's unholy rule; as such, Shakespeare took it from the English Chronicle and inserted it in his main political scene.

Further, into Macduff's reproaches of the supposedly vicious Malcolm, Shakespeare inserts an account of the forbears from whom he has degenerated; his father Duncan was "a most sainted king" and his mother one who "Oftener upon her knees, than on her feet, died every day she lived". This is Shakespeare's Duncan, not Holinshed's; while of Malcolm's mother nothing is known. Shakespeare has borrowed the saintliness from the description of Malcolm's wife, the English princess, St Margaret, who transmitted the blood of the Saxon line to the Scottish royal house, and whose little chapel still stands within the walls of Edinburgh Castle. It was she and Malcolm himself who rivalled each other in pious practices and holy living. But by putting this picture a generation earlier, Shakespeare has brought into the play yet another contrast with Macbeth and his fiend-like queen, whose land is described in terms of the plague:

> where nothing
> But who knows nothing, is once seen to smile:
> Where sighs, and groans, and shrieks that rend the air
> Are made, not mark'd: where violent sorrow seems
> A modern ecstasy: the dead man's knell,
> Is there scarce ask'd for who, and good men's lives
> Expire before the flowers in their caps,
> Dying, or ere they sicken. (iv, iii, 166–73)

As rightful heir Malcolm alone has the power to depose an anointed king, usurper though he be; but the conquest is almost unopposed. "The time is free." An immense feeling of relief surges up as Macduff appears on the battlements with these words. Malcolm, encompassed with his kingdom's pearl,[5] proceeds to inaugurate a new era by bestowing new honours. He thus fulfils his father's words that "signs of nobleness, like stars shall shine on all deservers". He also introduces the principle of feudal monarchy, with hereditary succession, and tenancy of the crown, which in fact Malcolm Canmore did institute in Scotland, following the unsuccessful attempts of his great-grandfather and grandfather, Kenneth II and Malcolm II.[6]

This particular theme, however, Shakespeare does not emphasize, and for good reason. The ancient succession of Scotland had been by tanistry, that is, the monarchy was elective within a small group of kinsmen, the descendants of Macalpine. In consequence, the king was almost as a matter of course assassinated by his successor, who chose the moment most favourable to himself to 'mak siccar' an inheritance that could never be regarded as assured. In spite of earlier attempts to make it hereditary, elective monarchy still persisted; by tanist law Macbeth had as good a claim as Duncan, and his wife a rather better one. By nominating Malcolm as his heir, the historic Duncan committed a provocative act which Macbeth might not unreasonably resent, and in Holinshed his real notions of murder are formed only at this point. Shakespeare did not wish Macbeth to have any such excuse for his deed. It must be unprovoked to give the full measure of pity and terror. Therefore by suppressing the conflict between tanistry and the hereditary principle, he was bound to slur over the full nature of Malcolm Canmore's innovations.[7]

On the contrary, the principle of hereditary succession is firmly emphasized by the prominence given to Banquo and his descendants, and in the cauldron scene Shakespeare has gratified the family pride of his royal patron by a pageant of his ancestors. Henry Paul has recently pointed out[8] that the Stewart line presented the striking picture of nine successive sovereigns in *lineal* descent the one from the other. This direct lineal descent of the crown was a matter of pride to

15

James, who referred to it in his speeches to Parliament and in his writings. Shakespeare's interest in genealogy had been amply shown in his English histories. Edward's seven sons, seven branches growing from one root, are recalled to mind by the family tree which has Banquo as its root—he so describes himself.

Banquo was a purely imaginary character, inserted into the Chronicle by Hector Boece to provide a proper ancestry for the Stewarts. Fleance's escape to Wales and his marriage with a Welsh princess 'explained' why the Stewarts did in fact come from the Welsh borders. But after 1603 the original expansion of the weird sisters' prophecy, whereby Banquo was hailed as father to a line of kings, was expanded still further, so that they also prophesied that his descendants should unite the kingdoms of England and Scotland. In the pageant of the three sybils given at St John's College, Oxford, in 1605, James and his family were greeted in this fashion, and moreover an endless progeny was promised him.[9] The show of the eight kings was an apotheosis of the Stewart line, and must have been staged with great grandeur. To a Jacobean audience it symbolized all the stability and order which they hoped from a settled succession. A family which had produced nine kings in lineal descent offered a fair hope of escape from those dynastic difficulties which Elizabeth's reign had made familiar. The eight phantoms are all "too like the spirit of Banquo". They are physical replicas of him, but in the last Henry Paul would see the person of Mary Queen of Scots, the eighth Stewart to wear the crown. At all events this scene would have a very powerful topical significance.

These two scenes, then, the cauldron scene and the scene in England, are the *political* highlights of the play. They are the scenes in which Shakespeare relied most heavily on his immediate sources—those he would start from. And they are the two scenes which would most particularly appeal to King James. They are also the least tragic in tone. One is spectacular, and the other, although, as I have said, it is much more poignant to the present age than to the previous one, is still in rather a different manner from the rest of the play. What have the theoretically well-justified dissimulations of this canny young man, this perfect looking-glass for princes, to do with the agonized visions of Inverness and Dunsinane? How do they fit one who has a father murdered as well as revenges to execute on the tyrant who popped in between the election and his hopes? Malcolm is own brother to that other canny young man, Harry Monmouth, who is likewise justified by all the text-books on government, including *Basilikon Doron*; but we are not moved. He is impersonal. The man is lost in the ruler. He may be *Vox Dei*; it means that he is merely *vox*.

Because of the close relation to source-material, the impersonal subject and the specific appeal to royal interest, it seems to me that these two scenes are probably the earliest to be written. I do not believe that Shakespeare, or any original writer, starts inevitably with Act I and ends with Act v. Nor do I think that, once submerged in his tragedy and well away from his sources, he would suddenly curb himself in mid-career and begin to treat these cooler matters. At the same time these scenes are too well articulated with the main plot to be additions, though small additions may have been made to them. The cauldron scene and the English scene are both in a quite laudatory, or at least a quite neutral sense, superficial. They belong to the top layer of the play.

The character of Lady Macbeth owes nothing to the Chronicle; it has been suggested that Shakespeare might have seen the MS. of William Stewart's *Buik of the Chroniclis of Scotland*, a metrical and expanded translation of Boece finished in 1535 which contains a few very crude hints on the behaviour of Donwald's wife during the murder of King Duff.[10] The resemblances seem to me negligible and unconvincing.

But a passage from the *Description of Scotland* which is prefixed to Holinshed's Chronicle and which to my knowledge has not hitherto been noted seems to be relevant. It is from chapter XIII:

...each woman would take intolerable pains to bring up and nourish her own children. They thought them furthermore not to be kindly fostered, except they were so well nourished after their births with the milk of their breasts as they were before they were born with the blood of their own bellies: nay, they feared lest they should degenerate and grow out of kind, except they gave them suck themselves, and eschewed strange milk, therefore in labour and painfulness they were equal [i.e. with the fighting men]....In these days also the women of our country were of no less courage than the men, for all stout maids and wives (if they were not with child) marched as well into the field as did the men, and so soon as the army did set forward, they slew the first living creature that they found, in whose blood they not only bathed their swords, but also tasted thereof with their mouths, with no less religion and assurance conceived, than if they had already been sure of some notable and fortunate victory.[11]

The intimate relation between tenderness and barbarity, suckling and bloodshed in this passage seems to me to give the fundamental character of Lady Macbeth as it is embodied in the most frightful of her speeches, that in which she invokes the spirits of murder to suck her breasts, and that in which she finally goads Macbeth:

> I have given suck, and know
> How tender 'tis to love the babe that milks me,
> I would, while it was smiling in my face,
> Have pluck'd my nipple from his boneless gums,
> And dash'd the brains out, had I so sworn
> As you have done to this.   (I, vii, 54–9)

Lady Macbeth is siren as well as fury. The tenderness of Macbeth for her is reciprocated; they are indeed one flesh. There are a number of parallels between her part and that of Webster's *White Divel*[12] which suggest that her seduction of Macbeth should not be too far removed from Vittoria's seduction of Brachiano in the manner of its playing. When Macbeth comes out of the death chamber she says two words: 'My husband?' The usual form of address is 'My thane' or 'My lord', but in this supreme moment she uses the more intimate, and for an Elizabethan the more unusual form.

The double crime of treason and murder is also deadly sin. In 1604 William Willymat, the translator of *Basilikon Doron* under the title of *A Prince's Looking-Glass*, followed it with an original work, *A Loyal Subject's Looking-Glass*, in which he described the prime causes of rebellion as pride, ambition and envy. All three animate Macbeth. "Pride can in no wise brook to be at command, and to submit himself willingly...to the obedience of magistrates, rulers and governors...be they never so well worthy of their place." Macbeth cannot brook

17

'the boy Malcolm', who has only been saved from captivity by the sergeant, should be nominated heir. Almost his last words are:

> I will not yield
> To kiss the ground before young Malcolm's feet.

The stripling—he should be of an age with his cousin, young Siward—provokes his pride; the Weird Sisters have stirred up ambition, always thought of as evil; and his very hunger for golden opinions makes him envy imperial dignity and the graces of kingship which he discerns in Duncan, and which he so vainly tries to reproduce. By the end of the play, Macbeth is accused of the other deadly sins also (IV, iii, 55–7)—in fact he is equated with the devil:

> Not in the legions
> Of horrid hell, can come a devil more damn'd
> In evils, to top Macbeth.

He is 'this fiend of Scotland', a 'hell-kite' and a 'hell-hound'.

In its treatment of the supernatural, the play shows the same subtle blending of a variety of material which is seen in the political theme; and it was again especially calculated to interest James, hero of *Newes from Scotland* and author of *Daemonologie*.

There was no real scepticism about witches. *Macbeth* comes at the end of a decade when the convictions for witchcraft in the Middlesex circuit reached their highest point. New statutes had been passed in 1604 reinforcing those of 1580, which made the consulting and feeding of spirits, the use of dead bodies as charms, and even unsuccessful efforts to harm by enchantment into indictable offences.[13]

It is rather surprising that before *Macbeth*, witches had appeared on the stage only in such harmless forms as Mother Bombie or the Wise Woman of Hogsdon. *Faustus* had been the only great tragedy to be based on the supernatural. The magician is a magnificent and powerful figure, a man of intellect. He enters into a formal pact with the devil and consciously chooses damnation; in return for the sale of his soul he obtains supernatural powers (*Daemonologie*, book I, chapter VI). Henceforth, though still free to repent, the devil coaxes and bullies him out of such wishes. The equal poise of Heaven and Hell that characterized the moralities is not maintained; the scales are weighed for Hell, dramatically speaking. The emissaries of Hell are more active, numerous and powerful than the emissaries of Heaven. The sinner, however, is led to will and choose his own damnation. He is never *possessed*.

Macbeth was the first play to introduce to the stage in a serious manner the rites and practices of contemporary witchcraft. The witch differed sharply from the magician, as King James observed (*Daemonologie*, book I, chapter III). William West of the Inner Temple thus distinguishes them in his *Symbolaeographie* (1594):

Soothsaying Wizards. Of this kind…be all those…which divine and foretell things to come and raise up evil spirits by certain superstitious and conceived forms of words. And unto such questions as be demanded of them do answer by voice, or else set before their eyes in glass, crystal stones, or rings, the pictures or images of things sought for.

[Witches]...shake the air with lightnings and thunder, to cause hail and tempests, to remove green corn or trees to an other place, to be carried of her familiar which hath taken upon him the deceitful shape of a goat, swine, or calf etc. into some mountain....And sometimes to fly upon a staff or fork, or some other instrument....[14]

Whilst Dee or Forman consorted with kings and princes, the witch was generally a poor, solitary, ignorant old woman. King James points out that magicians were learned and sought public glory; witches were unlearned and sought revenge. They blighted man and crops, were ugly and bearded, and went accompanied by a familiar. The more lurid practices of the continental sabbat are not recorded of English witches; though in *Daemonologie* and in the record of the North Berwick case, elaborate rituals are described, blasphemous as well as mischievous.

Shakespeare's play, though the first to deal with this topic seriously, was quickly followed by others. *Sophonisba* (1606) and *The Divil's Charter* (1607) were succeeded by a number of Chapman's plays introducing spirits, and in 1615 by Middleton's *Witch*, a song from which was incorporated in *Macbeth*. Jonson's *Masque of Queens*, with its celebrated antimasque of hags, was produced in 1609. As in *A Midsummer Night's Dream*, and later in *The Tempest*, Shakespeare created a new kind of supernatural drama and one which was very widely and generally imitated.

In all these plays, however, witches are used for spectacular and intermittent effects, and the marvellous elbows out the sinister. Marston and Jonson drew largely on classical sources. Hecate, in *The Witch*, is used to supply love charms and is surrounded by familiars but her influence is not decisive. Barnabe Barnes in *The Divil's Charter* is mainly indebted to *Faustus*, but the crimes of Alexander Borgia and Lucretia occasionally parallel those of Macbeth and Lady Macbeth, and the conjuring scene especially seems modelled on the cauldron scene, whilst Alexander is cheated by a riddle at the end, in much the same way as Macbeth.

In *Macbeth* Shakespeare combines many different traditions, so that the Weird Sisters, or Three Destinies of Holinshed become assimilated with the North Berwick coven in their malevolent rites, yet they also acquire something of the magician's power to raise and command spirits and to foretell the future. Shakespeare's witches, like those of North Berwick, appear capable of flying "through the fog and filthy air". They are able to sail in a sieve, to assume animal forms, and control the weather. All this Agnes Sampson and her coven claimed to do in their attempts to destroy the ship carrying King James from Denmark.[15] But Shakespeare's hags also have marks of the English witch—their beards, their animal familiars and their acts of petty revenge against the sailor and his wife. These were the things charged against many a poor old woman at the sessions. Their gift of prophecy expressed in riddles—the riddling form of words is not found in Holinshed—links them with such characters as Mother Bombie, or Erestus, the "white bear of England's wood" in *The Old Wives' Tale*. Incidentally, Rosalind, in the last act of *As You Like It*, makes her promises to the lovers in the riddling form proper to the Magician which she professes herself to be:

I will marry you, if ever I marry woman, and I'll be married tomorrow: I will satisfy you, if ever I satisfied man, and you shall be married tomorrow. I will content you, if what pleases you contents you, and you shall be married tomorrow.

(v, ii, 122–6)

The prophecies of the witches about Birnam Wood and the man not born of woman are sprigs of folklore which also recall the earlier comedies; for instance, Erestus's prophecy that Eumenides is to be released from enchantment by a dead man.[16]

On the other hand, they have powers superior to those of common witches. Bishop John Leslie called them devils disguised as women (*De Origine, Moribus et Rebus Gestis Scotorum*, Rome, 1578). They can vanish instantly like bubbles, which suggests a demonic power assuming and discarding human shape. They have no trace of any fear of or subjection to higher demonic forces; though the spirits raised in the cauldron scene are called 'our masters', yet the witches conjure them up and speak to them with authority, such authority as belongs to the magician like Faustus, the friar in *Bussy d'Ambois* and Owen Glendower. Macbeth, who sells his eternal jewel to the common enemy of man, is himself in Faustus's position, but he makes no formal compact, nor is he given any supernatural powers. He is tempted by rousing of his own worse instincts and led to natural crimes; but, on the other hand, he never renounces God and his baptism, as both witches and magicians were compelled to do. After the murder of Duncan there is no possibility of his going back. He has crossed the invisible boundary which cuts him off from his kind. His hand is against every man. He is no longer a member of the human community, and finally he sinks to the level of a hunted rogue animal.

Yet although Macbeth's career recalls a descent into hell, it is not presented openly as a descent into hell. In the end he finds himself deceived in the witches, as the witch or magician was so often deceived by the devil.[17] "Be these juggling fiends no more believ'd", he cries. In murdering Duncan, he committed mortal sin—the sin against the Holy Ghost as James called it in *Daemonologie* (book I, chapter II)—that is, he consciously and deliberately did that which he knew to be evil, and which he detested even as he did it. The act brings the punishment which he foresaw, he loses this clear sight, wades in blood so far that he is blinded and becomes in the end insensible even to the death of his wife.[18] But the overt theological issue is never bluntly put. Hence H. B. Charlton can deny any religious significance to *Macbeth*, while W. C. Curry, Helen Gardner and Hardin Craig, not to mention Roy Walker,[19] see the play as "essentially medieval and Christian". The Prince of Darkness is present only through the acts of his emissaries, but they, while in many ways recalling the realistic witch, are "creatures of another sort". I would not be prepared to say whether they are human or not; they are more recognizable as human in act I than in the later scenes, where they replace Holinshed's 'wizard', and have something of the devil's power of deceit.

Lady Macbeth's relation with the dark powers is more mysterious. Women were thought far more susceptible to demons than men, and were far more frequently accused of evil practices. King James put the proportion as high as twenty women to one man (*Daemonologie*, book II, chapter V). In her invocation to the spirits "that tend on mortal thoughts" Lady Macbeth offers them her breasts to be sucked and invites them to take possession of her body; this was as much as any witch could do by way of self-dedication. Professor Curry considers the sleep-walking scene to be evidence of possession, and if she did lay "self and violent hands" upon herself, Lady Macbeth committed the final act of Despair.

Neither Macbeth nor his wife has any defences. Though his conscience at first speaks clearly, he has no Good Angel as Faustus has. Banquo may pray to the merciful powers to restrain his cursed thoughts, Malcolm and Macduff appeal to Heaven, old Siward commit his dead son to the soldiery of God, but Macbeth lives in an amoral world of old wives' tales and riddles—except for that one vision of the pleading angels with their trumpet tongues, and heaven's cherubim horsed upon the sightless couriers of the air, which recalls Faustus's vision of Christ's blood streaming in the firmament.

The portents which accompany the death of Duncan, and foreshadow that of Banquo, are such as on the stage always appeared with the death of princes. The strange screams in the air and the horses that ate each other are developed from hints in Holinshed, but they are distinguished from other portents by the tone and colour of the language in which they are described. The thick darkness which hangs over the sky, the raven, owl and cricket's note are much less distinct than the fiery warriors who fought above the clouds in *Julius Caesar*. It is the thick night, the fog and filthy air, the smoke of hell which create the peculiar horror of this play, and the omens are chosen to accord. How quickly it rolls down on the sunlit battlements where the martlet flits, as a Scotch mist will roll from a mountain! Just as the witches are more horrible because we do not know what they are—it would be a relief to meet Mephistopheles—so the whole treatment of the supernatural in *Macbeth* is characterized by a potent and delicately controlled imprecision. Hell is murky. The creatures of *Macbeth*, like the ghost in *Hamlet*, are not susceptible of any one theoretical explanation, religious or natural.

Yet in the end justice, whether God's or Nature's, prevails. There is no direct intervention, but in the final vengeance the ingredients of the poisoned chalice are commended to the sinner's own lips. (This happens literally in *The Divil's Charter*, where Borgia is poisoned with his own wine: it also happens, of course, in *Hamlet*.) Macbeth, who had begun as Bellona's bridegroom, ends in the same role as Macdonwald, his head hacked off and put on a pole. (Did Macdonwald's head appear in the early scenes? According to Holinshed it was cut off.) The early description of Macbeth in battle which is given by the sergeant seems to me indubitably Shakespeare's. By the violence of it we are made unforgettably aware that bloodshed of itself is familiar to Macbeth—that his trade is hand-to-hand fighting. The physical side of Duncan's murder can cause him no qualms at all. Lady Macbeth, on the other hand, is not quite Holinshed's Valkyrie; perhaps she had not smelt blood before, and though she goes through the scene unflinchingly, she is haunted by the physical atrocity of it. To Macbeth, we may believe that the dastardly act of stabbing a sleeping old man was as instinctively repugnant as stabbing a kneeling man in the back was to Hamlet: "Look on't again, I dare not", he cries—he, who had unseamed men from the nave to the chaps.

It is here that we approach the deepest levels of the play and that we must leave external sources and seek within Shakespeare's own earlier work the foreshadowing of the terror and the pity which we feel. In the speeches of Macbeth, especially his five great speeches,[20] lies the heart of the mystery. They embody the experience which fundamentally gives rise to the play; and there are no sub-plots, no digressions to modify it.

Macbeth acts, according to Bradley, under a horrible compulsion; Dover Wilson imagines him following the air-drawn dagger in "a horrible smiling trance". The murder fascinates him as damnation fascinates Faustus. It is the inevitable, the irrevocable deed, after which he too dies in some sense:

> Had I but died an hour before this chance,
> I had liv'd a blessed time: for from this instant,
> There's nothing serious in mortality:
> All is but toys: renown and grace is dead,
> The wine of life is drawn.... (II, iii, 40–53)[21]

A period of intense and almost delirious anticipation is followed by complete collapse. There is one earlier picture of an "expense of spirit in a waste of shame", one earlier picture of conscious guilt calling in night and the creatures of night for aid, one act of physical violence followed by as swift a repentance, one equally dishonourable breach of hospitality and trust. It is the one to which Macbeth himself refers;

> Now o'er the one half-world
> Nature seems dead, and wicked dreams abuse
> The curtain'd sleep: witchcraft celebrates
> Pale Hecate's offerings: and wither'd murder,
> Alarum'd by his sentinel, the wolf,
> Whose howl's his watch, thus with his stealthy pace,
> With Tarquin's ravishing strides, towards his design
> Moves like a ghost. (II, i, 49–56)[22]

What is to be learnt by turning back to the sententious *Rape of Lucrece*, with its emblematic description of the heroine, its lengthy complaints and testament, its studied ornament and its formal indictment of Night, Time and Opportunity? Here, I think, are the emotional components (as distinct from the narrative components) of *Macbeth* lying separate, isolated, and more crudely and simply expressed. Tarquin's feelings before the deed, and Lucrece's feelings after it, are identical with the central core of feeling in *Macbeth*.

Night, Opportunity and a deceitful appearance are accessories to the deed. In her lament, Lucrece indicts these three. An atmosphere of tragic gloom and murk is diffused in the description of Tarquin's rising and stalking through the darkened house towards his victim. Like Macbeth, he tries to pray in the very act of entering her chamber and is startled to find that he cannot do it. There is a remote likeness to the physical horror of Duncan's corpse in the sight of Lucrece's body at the end, so ghastly inert in its great pool of blood

> Who like a late sack'd island vastly stood
> Bare and unpeopled, in this fearful flood. (1740–1)

But it is, above all, in the opening soliloquies of Tarquin that the likeness is apparent. Tarquin foresees the emptiness of his satisfaction, which Macbeth does not fully understand till after the deed; but the comment with which Tarquin's inward debate is introduced might serve as prologue to the later story.

> Those that much covet are with gain so fond,
> That what they have not, that which they possess
> They scatter and unloose it from their bond,
> And so by hoping more they have but less,
> Or gaining more, the profit of excess
>   Is but to surfeit, and such griefs sustain,
>   That they prove bankrupt in this poor-rich gain.

The aim of all is but to nurse the life,
With honour, wealth, and ease in waning age;
And in this aim there is such thwarting strife,
That one for all, or all for one we gage:
As life for honour, in fell battles rage,
   Honour for wealth, and oft that wealth doth cost
   The death of all, and altogether lost.

So that in venturing ill, we leave to be
The things we are, for that which we expect,
And this ambitious foul infirmity,
In having much torments us with defect
Of that we have: so then we do neglect
   The thing we have, and all for want of wit,
   Make something nothing, by augmenting it.   (134–54)

In his protracted debate with himself, Tarquin points out the shame to his family, his blood and his posterity, the transient nature of the gain (and here Macbeth echoes him):

Who buys a minute's mirth to wail a week?
Or sells eternity to get a toy?   (213–14)

He dreads the vengeance of Collatine even while he recognizes the ties of kinship and hospitality which bind them:

But as he is my kinsman, my dear friend,
The shame and fault finds no excuse nor end.   (237–8)

Finally he rejects the counsel of reason in words which anticipate Lady Macbeth's "'tis the eye of child-hood, That fears a painted devil":

Who fears a sentence or an old man's saw,
Shall by a painted cloth be kept in awe.   (244–5)

The crime which Tarquin commits, even more clearly, though not more truly, than Macbeth's, destroys the natural ties between him and the rest of the community. It is a sort of suicide. Both Macbeth and he commit a violence upon themselves from which they cannot recover. Examples have been known in the modern world where acts of sufficient violence will destroy the personality of the perpetrator; and even periods of acute nervous strain and danger, such as those to which combatants were subjected, will issue in nervous prostration and a feeling of complete emptiness of being. It is this identity between violence and self-violence (though in *The Rape of Lucrece*, the effects of the crime are given in the soliloquies of the victim) which a comparison of the two works reinforces as the central idea, the germ of the play. Macbeth's real victim is himself. Both *The Rape of Lucrece* and *Macbeth* reflect with very different degrees of skill a deep-seated and permanent experience; and the difference serves only to emphasize the unity of Shakespeare's art, the modifying and shaping power which his work as a whole seems to exert upon each of its parts. I think it is not fancy to say that *Macbeth* is the greater for being demonstrably by the hand that wrote *Othello*, or even the hand that wrote *Lucrece*; since the likeness which is discernible within such variety is proof that the play was written from the very depths of his mind and heart, and together with the multiplicity of sources which have furnished the subject of this paper, it gives a measure of the power, the intellectual and spiritual strength and pressure required, to weld them into one.

NOTES

1. The atmospheric strength of the chronicle is noted by Dover Wilson in the New Cambridge edition of *Macbeth* (Cambridge, 1947), p. xii. He quotes the earlier edition of Sir Herbert Grierson and J. C. Smith at this point in support of the Celtic atmosphere of the story. In a paper read at Cambridge in November 1950, Mrs N. K. Chadwick suggested that the earliest chronicle, Wyntoun's, incorporates material from lost Celtic sagas on Macbeth, particularly in the parts relating to the supernatural. She bases this on changes in the style, indicating a Celtic original. There is an independent Norse saga of Macbeth.

2. *Basilikon Doron*, and *The true lawe of free monarchies* (Edinburgh, 1597, 1598).

3. *Ed. cit.* pp. xxxi–xxxii.

4. Hardin Craig, *An Interpretation of Shakespeare* (New York, 1948).

5. Henry Paul points out in his article, 'The Imperial Theme in *Macbeth*' (*Adams Memorial Studies*, ed. J. G. McManaway and others, Washington, 1948, pp. 253–68), that the *pearls* set in the base of an imperial diadem represented the several dependent fiefs (*loc. cit.* p. 264). What follows in my text is indebted to this valuable article.

6. St Margaret, Malcolm's wife, and a strong influence in the shaping of his policy, obtained from the Pope the privilege that Scottish kings should be anointed (i.e. hallowed) at their coronation.

7. It is melancholy to note that Donalbain returned from Ireland to the Isles and (after Malcolm's death) slew his nephew, David, but was in turn succeeded by another of Malcolm's sons. With this one interval, the line of Malcolm Canmore retained the throne.

8. *Loc. cit.* p. 258.

9. It has been much disputed whether Shakespeare knew this pageant or not. Henry Paul thinks he did.

10. See Dover Wilson, *ed. cit.* p. xvii, for a summary of the material.

11. *The Description of Scotland*, chapter xiii (translated from the Latin of Hector Boethius by William Harison, and prefixed to Holinshed's *Historie of Scotland*, 1577). As in the other quotations the spelling has been modernized.

12. Vittoria's "Terrify babes, my Lord, with painted devils" and the words of Flamineo about her, "If woman do breed man, She ought to teach him manhood", recall respectively "tis the eye of child-hood That fears a painted devil" and "Bring forth men-children only". The figure of the great lady, great in wickedness, was popular on the Jacobean stage. Lucrezia Borgia in *The Divil's Charter* also recalls Lady Macbeth in her laments and swoon over the husband she has slain, her invocation of the furies and her careful concealment of the murder by staging a mock suicide.

13. C. H. L. Ewen, *Witch Hunting and Witch Trials* (London, 1929), pp. 19–21, 31. I am indebted for this reference and for much general information on the subject of demonology to Mrs Florence Trefethan.

14. Quoted Ewen, *op. cit.* p. 23.

15. See *Newes from Scotland*, 1591 (reprinted with King James's *Daemonologie* in the Bodley Head Quartos, London, 1924).

16. *The Old Wives' Tale* (*The Works of George Peele*, ed. A. H. Bullen, vol. i, p. 323).

17. In the words of King James (*Daemonologie*, book i, chapter v)—which seem to be recalled by Banquo in i, iii—the devil tries "to make himself so to be trusted in these little things, that he may have the better commodity thereafter, to deceive in the end with a trick once for all; I mean the everlasting perdition of their soul and body". Cf. the deception of Alexander Borgia, unmasked at the end of *The Divil's Charter*.

18. This insensibility is contrasted with the Christian stoicism of Macduff and old Siward, who endure their bereavements courageously, not barbarously.

19. H. B. Charlton, *Shakespearian Tragedy* (Cambridge, 1948); W. C. Curry, *Shakespeare's Philosophical Patterns* (Baton Rouge, 1937); Helen Gardner, 'Milton and the Tragedy of Damnation' in *English Studies*, 1948, ed. F. P. Wilson (London, 1948); Hardin Craig, 'Motivation in Shakespeare's Choice of Materials', *supra* pp. 31–2; Roy Walker, *The Time is Free* (London, 1949).

20. *Macbeth*, I, vii, 1–28; II, i, 31–64; III, ii, 13–26, 46–53; v, iii, 40–53; v, v, 17–28.

21. Cf. the line below, from *Lucrece*: "Who...sells eternity to get a toy?" and the lassitude of Cleopatra at Antony's death:

> The odds is gone,
> And there is nothing left remarkable
> Beneath the visiting moon.   (IV, xv, 66–8)

22. It may be noted that this atmosphere is recalled again in Iachimo's speech over the sleeping Imogen: night, 'our *Tarquin*' with his stealthy tread, the crickets' cry (*Cymbeline*, II, ii, 11–14).

THE CRIMINAL AS TRAGIC HERO: DRAMATIC METHODS

BY

ROBERT B. HEILMAN

I

The difficulties presented by the character of Macbeth—the criminal as tragic hero—have led some critics to charge Shakespeare with inconsistency, others to seek consistency by viewing the initial Macbeth as in some way morally defective,[1] and still others to normalize the hero by viewing the final Macbeth as in some way morally triumphant. Perhaps a recollection of Lascelles Abercrombie's enthusiastic phrase, 'the zest and terrible splendour of his own unquenchable mind' (1925), and of Wilson Knight's comparable 'emerges at last victorious and fearless'[2] (1930), helped stir L. C. Knights to complain (1933) that 'the critics have not only sentimentalized Macbeth—ignoring the completeness with which Shakespeare shows his final identification with evil—but they have slurred the passages in which the positive good is presented by means of religious symbols'.[3] Even after this, so unflighty an editor as Kittredge could say that Macbeth 'is never greater than in the desperate valour that marks his end'.[4] On the other hand, the editor of a *Macbeth* meant for schools describes Macbeth as a 'bold, exacting and presumptuous criminal, . . . bent on destruction for destruction's sake', 'the champion of evil', 'a monster', giving 'the impression . . . of some huge beast who . . . dies lashing out at everyone within range'.[5] But if intemperateness of eulogy or condemnation is exceptional, the opposing impulses are not altogether reconciled; if to many critics Macbeth is damned, there is hardly consensus about either the way down or the mitigating circumstances or how good the bad man is. 'Damned, but' might be a title for an anthology of critical essays.

The problem of character, which is no more than quickly sketched by this sampling of judgments, becomes intertwined with the problem of generic placement, a standard, though rarely decisive, evaluating procedure. If the play changes from the study of a complex soul to the history of good men's victory over a criminal and tyrant, has it not dropped from the level of high tragedy to that of political melodrama? This seems harsh, and we can evade it either by discovering unmelodramatic complications in Macbeth as king (a method approached by Neilson and Hill when they acknowledge that Macbeth 'proved a desperately wicked man' but add, with mild confidence, '. . . we are reassured that he was more than the mere butcher the avenging Malcolm not unnaturally calls him'),[6] or by minimizing the importance of character and insisting that the play is a great dramatic poem (as in that anti-Bradleyism which can be traced at least from Knights's 1933 essay). When we look, as many critics do, at the poetic-dramatic structure, we find, among other things, that the nadaism of Macbeth's 'Tomorrow and tomorrow and tomorrow' speech is not Shakespeare's but Macbeth's and that the play contains numerous images of good kingship and affirmative life; Macbeth is regularly in contrast with the norms of order and hope. The trouble with abstracting a meaning—'Crime doesn't pay' or 'The way of transgressors is hard'—and regarding character as principally a buttress of that meaning[7] is that it has consequences for the placement of drama. Kenneth Muir faces the consequences when he says, 'We may, indeed, call *Macbeth* the greatest of morality plays . . .'.[8] However, Muir is understandably diffident about the term 'morality play'; so he not only says 'greatest' but adds a weighty series of codicils intended to cushion to the utmost, or even counteract, the implicit demotion from 'tragedy' to 'morality play'.

The critical uneasiness with the character of Macbeth is different from the usual feelings—uncertainty, attentiveness, curiosity, passion to examine, and so on—stirred by an obscure or elusive character, because it springs from a disturbing sense of discrepancy not evoked, for instance, by Shakespeare's other tragic heroes. We expect the tragic protagonist to be an expanding character, one who grows in awareness and spiritual largeness; yet Macbeth is to all intents a contracting character, who seems to discard large areas of consciousness as he goes, to shrink from multilateral to unilateral being (we try to say it isn't so by deflating the Macbeth of Acts I and II and inflating the Macbeth of Acts IV and V). The diminishing personality is of course not an anomaly in literature, whether in him we follow a gradual decrease of moral possibility or discover an essential parvanimity, but this we expect in satire (Fielding's Blifil, Austen's Wickham, Meredith's Sir Austin Feverel, Eliot's Lydgate), not tragedy. This source of uneasiness with Macbeth, however, is secondary; the primary source is a technical matter, Shakespeare's remarkable choice of point of view—that of this ambitious man who, in Muir's words that sum up the contracting process, 'becomes a villain'. We have to see through his eyes, be in his skin; for us, this is a great breach of custom, and in the effort at accommodation we do considerable scrambling. When we share the point of view of Hamlet, we experience the fear of evil action and of evil inaction; when we share the point of view of Othello and Lear, we experience passionate, irrational action whose evil is not apprehended or foreseen; but when we share the point of view of Macbeth, we have to experience the deliberate choice of evil. Hence a disquiet altogether distinguishable from the irresoluteness of mind before, let us say, some apparent contradictions in Othello.

The problem is like that which usually comes up when readers[9] must adopt the point of view of a character in whom there are ambiguities. Unless structure is based on contrasts, point of view ordinarily confers authority; but discomforts, which invariably lead to disagreements, arise when authority apparently extends to matters which, on aesthetic, rational, psychological, or moral grounds, the reader finds it difficult to countenance.[10] 'Disagreements', of course, implies studious recollection in tranquillity, or rather, untranquillity; what we are concerned with in this discussion is the immediate, unanalysed imaginative experience which precedes the effort to clarify or define. We are assuming that the person experiencing *Macbeth* is naturally carried into an identification with Macbeth which, if incomplete, is still more far-reaching than that with anyone else in the play. This should be a safe working assumption,[11] whatever the modifications of sensibility that qualify the immediate unanalysed experience and hence lead to alternative explanations of Macbeth in retrospect. Surely Muir is right in saying of our response to Macbeth that 'we are tempted and suffer with him'.[12]

Behind our condemnation of trivial literature, whether we call it 'sentimental', 'meretricious', or something else, lies the sense that the characters whom for the moment we become give us an inadequate or false sense of reality, call into action too few of our human potentialities. Hence 'tragedy' tends not simply to designate a genre, in which there may be widely separated levels of excellence, but to become an honorific term: it names a noble enterprise, the action of a literary structure which compels us to get at human truth by knowing more fully what we are capable of—'knowing', not by formal acts of cognition but by passing imaginatively through revelatory experiences. In a morality we see a demonstration of what happens; in tragedy we act out what happens, undergoing a kind of kinaesthetic initiation into conduct we would not ordinarily acknowledge as belonging to us. The problem is how far this process of illuminating induction can go without running into resistance that impedes or derails the tragic experience, without exciting self-protective counter-measures such as retreating from tragic co-existence with the hero to censorious observation of him from a distant knoll.[13] *Macbeth* at least permits this way out by its increasingly extensive portrayal, in Acts IV and V, of the counterforces whom we see only as high-principled seekers of justice. Do we, so to speak, defect to them because Macbeth, unlike Lear and Othello, moves into a greater darkness in which we can no longer discern our own lineaments? Do we, then, turn tragedy into melodrama or morality?

II

That, of course, is a later question. The prior question is the mode of our relationship with Macbeth when he kills Duncan; here we have to consent to participation in a planned murder, or at least tacitly accept our capability of committing it. The act of moral imagination is far greater, as we have seen, than that called for by the germinal misdeeds of Lear or the murder by Othello, since these come out of emotional frenzies where our tolerance, or even forgiveness, is so spontaneous that we need not disguise our kinship with those who realize in action what we act in fantasy. Yet technically Shakespeare so manages the situation that we become Macbeth, or at least assent to complicity with him, instead of shifting to that simple hostility evoked by the melodramatic treatment of crime. We accept ourselves as murderers, so to speak, because we also feel the strength of our resistance to murder. The initial Macbeth has a fullness of human range that makes him hard to deny; though a kind of laziness makes us naturally vulnerable to the solicitation of some narrow-gauge characters, we learn by experience and discipline to reject these (heroes of cape and sword, easy masters of the world, pure devils, simple victims); and correspondingly we are the more drawn in by those with a large store of human possibilities, good and evil. Macbeth can act as courageous patriot (I, ii, 35 ff.), discover that he has dreamed of the throne ('... why do you start...?'—I,iii, 51), entertain the 'horrid image' of murdering Duncan (I, iii, 135), be publicly rewarded by the king (I, iv), be an affectionate husband (I, v), survey, with anguished clarity, the motives and consequences of the imagined deed; reject it; feel the strength of his wife's persuasion, return to 'this terrible feat' (I, vii, 80); undergo real horrors of anticipation (II, i, 31 ff.) and of realization that he has actually killed Duncan (II, ii, 14 ff.). Here is not a petty scoundrel but an extraordinary man, so capacious in feeling and motive as to have a compelling representativeness; we cannot adopt him selectively, feel a oneness with some parts of him and reject others; we become the murderer as well as the man who can hardly tolerate, in prospect or retrospect, the idea of murder. The suffering is so great that the act is hedged about with penance; unless we are neurotic, we cannot pay such a price

28

without earning it; murder belongs, as it were, to normalcy—to us in our normalcy. Further-more, the anguish is so powerful and protracted, and the 'terrible feat' so quickly done, that it marks only a brief failure of moral governance; we seem to sacrifice only a mite of the sentience that we instinctively attribute to ourselves. That, too, after solicitations whose power we feel directly: 'Vaulting Ambition', indeed, but also challenges to our manly courage, the promise of security, and, behind these, the driving strength of another soul not easy to disappoint or even, when the other speaks for a part of ourselves, to resist. These persuasions, in turn, are a supple-ment to 'supernatural soliciting' (I, iii, 130), to 'fate and metaphysical aid' (I, v, 26). Finally, Shakespeare affords the reader one more aid in accepting his alliance with the murderer: that alteration of ordinary consciousness that enhances the persuasiveness of deviant conduct by the 'good man'. From the first prophetic phrases Macbeth has been 'rapt', a word applied to him thrice (I, iii, 57, 142; I, v, 5), and when the knocking is heard Lady Macbeth adjures him,

> Be not lost
> So poorly in your thoughts;   (II, ii, 71–2)

there are also his dagger-vision speech before the murder (II, i, 33 ff.), and after it the hallucina-tory impressions that make Lady Macbeth use the word 'brainsickly' (II, ii, 46). The note of 'unsound mind' helps make the murderer 'one of us', to use Conrad's term, rather than a criminal-outsider.

If it be a function of tragedy, as we have suggested, to amplify man's knowledge of himself by making him discover, through imaginative action, the moral capabilities to which he may ordinarily be blind, then Shakespeare, in the first two acts of *Macbeth*, has so managed his tools that the function is carried out superlatively well. He leads the reader on to accept himself in a role that he would hardly dream of as his. If it be too blunt to say that he becomes a murderer, at least he feels murderousness to be as powerful as a host of motives more familiar to conscious-ness. Whether he knows it or not, he knows something more about himself. It may be that 'knows' takes us too far into the realm of the impalpable, but to use it is at least to say meta-phorically that the reader remains 'with' Macbeth instead of drifting away into non-participa-tion and censure. Shakespeare's dramaturgic feat should not be unappreciated.

III

That behind him, Shakespeare moves ahead and takes on a still greater difficulty: the maintaining of identity, his and ours, with a character who, after a savage initial act, goes on into other monstrosities, gradually loses more of his human range, contracts, goes down hill.[14] Surely this is the most demanding technical task among the tragedies. Othello and Lear both grow in knowledge; however reluctantly and incompletely, they come into a sense of what they have done, and advance in powers of self-placement. With them we have a sense of recovery, which paradoxically accompanies the making of even destructive discoveries. Renouncing blindness is growth. Macbeth does not attract us into kinship in this way; his own powers of self-recognition seem to have been squandered on the night of the first murder and indirectly in the dread before Banquo's ghost. Nevertheless there are passages in which he has been felt to be placing and judging himself. There may indeed be something of tragic self-knowledge in the man who says that he has 'the gracious Duncan . . . murder'd' and

mine eternal jewel
Given to the common enemy of man;   (III, i, 65, 67–8)

yet he is not saying 'I have acted evilly', much less 'I repent of my evil conduct', but rather, 'I have paid a high price—and for what? To make Banquo the father of kings.' Macbeth is not so simple and crude as not to know that the price is high, but his point is that for a high price he ought to be guaranteed the best goods; and in prompt search of the best goods he elaborates the remorselessly calculating rhetoric by which he inspirits the murderers to ambush Banquo and Fleance. Again, he can acknowledge his and Lady Macbeth's nightmares and declare buried Duncan better off than they, but have no thought at all of the available means of mitigating this wretchedness; the much stronger motives appear in his preceding statement 'We have scorch'd the snake, not kill'd it' and his following one, 'O, full of scorpions is my mind . . . that Banquo, and his Fleance, lives' (III, ii, 13, 36–7). The serpents of enmity and envy clearly have much more bite than the worm of conscience.

I am in blood
Stepp'd in so far   (III, iv, 136–7)

encourages some students to speak as if Macbeth were actuated by a sense of guilt, but since no expectable response to felt guilt inhibits his arranging, very shortly, the Macduff murders, it seems more prudent to see in these words only a technical summary of his political method. In 'the sere, the yellow leaf' lines Macbeth's index of the deprivations likely to afflict him in later years (v, iii, 23 ff.) suggests to some readers an acute moral awareness; it seems rather a regretful notice of social behaviour, such as would little trouble the consciousness of a man profoundly concerned about the quality of his deeds and the state of his soul. Finally, in Macbeth's battlefield words to Macduff—

my soul is too much charg'd
With blood of thine already—   (v, viii, 5–6)

some critics have detected remorse. It may be so, but in the general context of actions of a man increasingly apt in the sanguinary and freed from refinement of scruple, there is much to be said for the suggestion that he is 'rationalizing his fear';[15] possibly, too, he is unconsciously placating the man who has most to avenge and of whom the First Apparition has specifically warned him (IV, i, 71).

Since different Shakespearians have been able to find in such passages a continuance of genuine moral sensitivity in Macbeth, it is possible that for the non-professional reader they do indeed belong to the means by which a oneness with Macbeth is maintained. If so, then we have that irony by which neutral details in an ugly man's portrait have enough ambiguity to help win a difficult assent to him. However, a true change of heart is incompatible with a retention of the profits secured by even the temporarily hardened heart, and the fact is that once Macbeth has become king, all of his efforts are directed to hanging on to the spoils of a peculiarly obnoxious murder. Shakespeare has chosen to deal not only with an impenitent, though in many ways regretful, man, but with one whose crime has been committed only to secure substantial worldly advantages (in contrast with the wrongs done by Lear and Othello). Perhaps what the play

30

'says' is that such a crime has inevitable consequences, that worldly profit—goods, honour, power—is so corrupting that, once committed to it, the hero can never really abjure it, can never really repent and seeks ways of spiritual alteration, though he may cry out against the thorns and ugliness of the road he cannot leave.[16] However far such a theory can be carried, it is plain that Macbeth, once he has taken the excruciatingly difficult first step on the new route, discovers in himself the talents for an unsurrenderable athleticism in evil.

The artist's problem is that for a reader to accompany such a character and to share in his intensifying depravity might become intolerable; the reader might simply flee to the salvation of condemning the character. This does not happen. For, having chosen a very difficult man to establish our position—to give us shoes and skin and eyes and feeling—Shakespeare so manages the perspective that we do not escape into another position. As with all his tragic heroes, Shakespeare explores the point of view of self, the self-defending and self-justifying motions of mind and heart; alert as we are to self-protectiveness in others, we still do not overtly repudiate that of Macbeth. That is, Macbeth finds ways of thinking about himself and his dilemmas that we find congenial, and, even more than that, ways of feeling which we easily share. The dramatist can rely somewhat, of course, on that ambiguous sympathy with the criminal that human beings express in various ways; even an artist who is not romanticizing a criminal can count on it up to a point if he protects it against counter feelings. Suppose, for instance, that we had seen a great deal of Duncan at Macbeth's castle or that the murder were done on the stage or that Macbeth did not undergo the agonies depicted in II, ii; he would already have lost his role as erring humanity, and we ours as secret sharer. Suppose, also, that he then took the throne by blunt force, or were grossly shameless, or rapped out lies which everyone knew to be lies. But he does not drive us away by such methods; instead, our murderer is a man who suffers too much, as it were, really to be a murderer; he agonizes more than he antagonizes. After the murder, we next see him in a painfully taxing and challenging position—the utter necessity of so acting in public, at a moment of frightful public calamity, that neither his guilt will be revealed nor his ambition threatened. The pressure on him shifts to us, who ought to want him caught right there. Can he bring it off? Can we bring it off? In some way we become the terribly threatened individual, the outnumbered solitary antagonist; further, our own secret self is at stake, all our evil, long so precariously covered over, in danger of being exposed, and we of ruin. But we miraculously come through, our terrible anxiety somehow transmuted to strength under fire; we say the right things ('Had I but died an hour before this chance', II, iii, 89), have the presence of mind to be carried away by 'fury' and kill the chamberlains and turn suspicion on them, and still to 'repent' the fury (105). Relief, perhaps triumph. This statement may require more delicacy and precision, but it should indicate the way in which Shakespeare instinctively approaches the task of enticing us into collusion. We remain the murderer in part because the pressure of other motives makes us forget that we are. What we forget we do not deny.

Macbeth is in danger of degenerating from Everyman into monster, that is, of pushing us from unspoken collusion to spoken judgment, when he coolly plots against Banquo. But Shakespeare moves Macbeth quickly into a recital of motives and distresses that invite an assent of feeling. Macbeth's important 25-line soliloquy (III, i, 47–71) is in no sense a formal apologia, but it has the effect of case-making by the revelation of emotional urgencies whose force easily comes home to us. There are three of these urgencies. The first is fear, that especial kind of fear that derives from insecurity: '. . . to be safely thus' (48) is a cry so close to human needs that it can make us forget that the threat to safety is made by justice. The fear is of Banquo, a man of 'dauntless temper', of 'wisdom' (51, 52); we can credit ourselves with Macbeth's ability and willingness to discriminate at the same time that, unless we make an improbable identification with Banquo, we can enter into the lesser man's sense of injury and his inclination to purge himself of second-class moral citizenship. The second great appeal is that to the horror of being in a cul de sac, of feeling no continuity into something beyond the present: all that we have earned will be nothing if we have but a 'fruitless crown', 'a barren sceptre', 'No son' (60–3). It is the Sisters that did this; 'they' are treating us unfairly, inflicting a causeless deprivation. Our Everyman's share of paranoia is at work. Yet the price has been a high one ('vessel of my peace', loss of 'mine eternal jewel'); it is as if a bargain had been unfulfilled, and we find ourselves sharing the third emotional pressure—resentment at a chicanery of events which need not be borne.

The anxiety in the face of constant threats, the pain at being cut off from the future, the bitterness of the wretched bargain—these emotions, since they may belong to the most upright life, tend to inhibit our making a conscious estimate of the uprightness of the man who experiences them. This may be a sufficient hedge against our splitting away from Macbeth when he is whipping up the Murderers against Banquo. But since Macbeth can trick us into the desire to 'get away with it', or into discovering that we can have this desire, it may be that even the subornation of murder evokes a distant, unidentified, and unacknowledgeable compliance. Here the appeal would be that of executive dispatch and rhetorical skill in a difficult cause; it is satisfying to use against another the method before which one has been defenceless earlier, the appeal to manliness (91 ff.), to hint the grave danger to oneself (115–17), to claim a meritorious abstention from 'bare-fac'd power' (118), though the power is legitimate. Then quickly, before we have time to cast off the spell, to catch ourselves tricked into a silent partnership in crime and to start backing away from it, we are enthralled in another way: again, this time with both Macbeth and Lady Macbeth, the terrible fear, the sense of constant menace, the 'affliction of these terrible dreams', the 'torture of the mind' (III, ii, 18, 21). Afflictions and tortures: we have our own, and we do not stop, step to one side, and think that ours are more just and noble than those of the wretched royal pair. Macbeth's language, in a brilliant touch, even makes the usurpers weak victims, such as we sometimes like to be: threatening them is a 'snake', cut in two, but reuniting to extend the 'danger', against which we offer but 'poor malice', that is, feeble opposition (14–15). Here is one of the subtler of the series of verbal and dramatic means by which we are held 'with' Macbeth and the queen; we are with them as long as we do not turn and say, 'But what do you expect?' And as long as we do not say that, we have not shifted to the posture invited by melodrama and morality play.

At the banquet scene the courtesy and breeding of the host and hostess hardly seem that of vulgar criminals, from whom we would quickly spring away into our better selves. But before the Ghost appears, Macbeth learns of the escape of Fleance, and he speaks words that appeal secretly to two modes of responsiveness. He introduces the snake image from III, ii, 14: as for Banquo, 'There the grown serpent lies', but then there's Fleance:

> the worm that's fled
> Hath nature that in time will venom breed. (III, iv, 29–30)

It is not that we rationally accept Macbeth's definition of father and son, but that we share his desperateness as destined victim; and his image for the victimizing forces, as long as it is not opposed openly in the context, is one to evoke the fellowship of an immemorial human fear. This, however, tops off a subtler evocation of sympathy, Macbeth's

> I am cabin'd, cribb'd, confin'd, bound in
> To saucy doubts and fears.
> (24–5)

The new image for fear, which we have already been compelled to feel, is peculiarly apt and constraining: it brings into play the claustrophobic distress that can even become panic. We do not pause for analysis, stand off, and say, 'It is the claustrophobia of crime'; rather the known phobia maintains our link with the criminal. Then, of course, the moral responsiveness implied by the appearance of the Ghost and by Macbeth's terror make a more obvious appeal, for here the traditional 'good man' is evident. Not only does he again become something of a victim, but the royal pair draw us into their efforts to save a situation as dangerous as it is embarrassing and humiliating. They are in such straits that we cannot now accuse them, much less triumph over them. Macbeth's demoralizing fear, finally, works in a paradoxical way: fear humanizes the warrior and thus brings us closer to him, while his inevitable reaction from it into almost hyperbolic courage, with its conscious virility ('Russian bear', 'Hyrcan tiger', etc., 99 ff.), strikes a different chord of consent. From now on until the end, indeed, Macbeth is committed to a bravery, not unspontaneous but at once compensating and desperate—a bravura of bravery—that it is natural for us to be allied with.

The danger point is that at which the admired bravery and its admired accompaniment, resolution (such as appears in the visit to the Witches, IV, i), are distorted into the ruthlessness of the Macduff murders. Here we are most likely to be divorced from Macbeth, to cease being actors of a role and become critics of it. At any rate, Shakespeare takes clear steps to 'protect' Macbeth's position. That 'make assurance double sure' (IV, i, 83) has become a cliché is confirmatory evidence that the motive is well-nigh universal; getting rid of Macduff becomes almost an impersonal safety measure, additionally understandable because of the natural wish to 'sleep in spite of thunder' (86). We come close to pitying his failure to grasp the ambiguity of the oracles, for we can sense our own naiveté and wishful thinking at work; and his disillusionment and emptiness on learning that Banquo's line will inherit the throne, are not so alien to us that Macbeth's retaliatory passion is unthinkable. Shakespeare goes ahead with the risk: we see one of the cruel murders, and the next time Macbeth appears, he is hardly attractive either in his almost obsessive denying of fear (V, iii, 1–10) or in his letting his tension explode in pointless abuse of his servant, partly for fearfulness (11–18). Still, the impulses are ones we can feel. Now, after Macbeth has been on the verge of breaking out into the savage whom we could only repudiate, things take a different turn, and Macbeth comes back toward us as more than a loathsome criminal. He is 'sick at heart' (19)—words that both speak to a kindred feeling and deny that the speaker is a brute. He meditates on approaching age (22 ff.), with universality of theme and dignity of style teasing us into a fellowship perhaps strengthened by respect for the intellectual candour with which he lists the blessings he has forfeited. Above all he has a desperately sick wife: pressed from without, still he must confer with the doctor and in grief seek remedies for a 'mind diseas'd', 'a rooted sorrow', 'that perilous stuff / Which weighs upon the heart'

(40–5). Shakespeare makes him even extend this humane concern, either literally or with a wry irony that is still not unattractive, to the health of Scotland:

> find her disease,
> And purge it to a sound and pristine health.   (51–2)

Along with all of the troubles that he meets, more often than not with sad equanimity, he must also face crucial desertions: 'the thanes fly from me' (49). Like us all, he tells his troubles to the doctor. He has become an underdog, quite another figure from the cornered thug, supported by a gang of sinister loyalty, that he might be. This athlete in evil, as we called him earlier, has had to learn endurance and endure, if we may be forgiven, the loneliness of the long-distance runner. Against such solitude we hardly turn with reproof.

Macbeth opened the scene crying down fear; he goes on with three more denials of fear, one at the end (32, 36, 59); now we are able to see in the repetition an effort to talk down deep misgivings, and the hero again approximates Everyman, ourselves. When Macbeth next appears, just before the battle, it is the same: he opens and closes the scene literally or implicitly denying fear, even though the prophecy of his end seems miraculously fulfilled (v, v, 1–15, 51–2). Meanwhile the queen's death is reported, and the warrior, moved but finely controlled, turns grief into contemplation, with the seductiveness of common thought in uncommon language. The closing battle scene is a series of denials of fear, appealing to both pity and admiration. Some details are instinctively ingratiating. 'They have tied me to a stake; I cannot fly' (v, vii, 1)— oneself as the victim of others bent on cruel sport. 'Why should I play the Roman fool . . . ?' (v, viii, 1)—no moral retreat, no opting out of adversity. 'I will not yield' (27)—the athlete's last span of endurance, fight against all odds.

IV

My intention has been, not to offer a full study of Macbeth or a fresh account of his moral alteration, not to argue that he is a worse man than some have thought (though some analyses seem not to catch what Knights called 'the completeness [of] his final identification with evil') or a better man than other men have thought (though he is remarkably endowed with aspects of personality not ordinarily expected in a man committed to evil), but to describe the apparent impact made upon the imagination by certain deeds, thoughts, and feelings of his. Since there is hardly a need to demonstrate that Macbeth is a villain and that villains ordinarily repel us, the emphasis has naturally fallen upon those elements in him that tend to elicit, in whatever degree, fellow-feeling, pity, favour, or even admiration. Macbeth possibly establishes a subtle kinship by setting in motion certain impulses which we would rather not admit—anomalous siding with the criminal, aggressive ambition, envy, the pleasure of getting away with it (which includes leaving the 'it' unexamined). More frequently the appeal to allegiance is that of states or situations which are neutral in that they may come to good or bad men but which, without analysing the merits of the figure involved, we find it difficult not to fear or pity—the threat of exposure, the anxieties of a perilous position, relentless enclosure by men and circumstances, nightmares and insomnia of whatever origin, the pressing need for greater safety, the pain of miscalculation and the gnawing sense of a bad bargain, any enlargement of the penalties of advanced age, desertion, the unequal struggle, the role of the underdog. Finally, and more important, Macbeth early gives every sign of having a conscience, and later he exhibits qualities and abilities that normally elicit respect or admiration—resourcefulness under severely taxing stresses, readiness for intolerable difficulties, resolution, the philosophic cast of mind, endurance, bravery.

If the general demonstration, as it is summarized here, has merit, it opens the way to several other points. For one thing, it should help explain some rather enthusiastic accounts of Macbeth: that which binds us to him, either the painfulness of what he endures or the qualities that he shares with men we admire, so overwhelms the sense of the ruthless tyrant that we either let this slip out of operative consciousness or take it for granted as not requiring further discussion, and proceed then to erect a rational form for all the feelings of kinship or approval. Shakespeare has so thoroughly attacked the problem of keeping a villain from being a mere villain that at times it has apparently been easy to lose sight of his villainy. On the other hand, the endowing of Macbeth with the power to attract fellow-feeling and even approval makes it unlikely that 'the sympathies of the audience are switched to his enemies'.[17] This is a crucial matter. For if such a switch does take place, then the play does not hold us in an essentially tragic engagement, but carries us into a relationship like that with *Richard III* (a play often used to illustrate *Macbeth*).

To be convinced of Macbeth's retention of our sympathy may seem to imply a denial of our sympathy to Malcolm, Macduff, and the conquering party. By no means: obviously we share their passions whenever these control the action, and we may even cheer them on. Yet we do not remain fixedly and *only* with them, as we do with Richmond and his party in *Richard III*, and with such forces in all dramas with a clearly melodramatic structure. When the anti-Macbeth leaders occupy the stage, we are unable not to be at one with them; but the significant thing is that when his point of view is resumed, Macbeth again draws us back, by the rather rich means that we have examined, into our old collusion. After III, vi, when we first see committed opposition to Macbeth ('. . . this our suffering country, / Under a hand accurs'd !'—48–9), the two sides alternate on the stage until they come together in battle. In one scene we have the rather easy, and certainly reassuring, identification with the restorers of order; in the next, the strange, disturbing emotional return to the camp of the outnumbered tyrant. We move back and forth between two worlds and are members of both. As a contemporary novelist says of a character who is watching fox and hounds, 'She wanted it to get away, yet when she saw the hounds she also wanted them to catch it'.[18]

Macbeth, in other words, has a complexity of form which goes beyond that normally available to melodrama and morality play, where the issue prevents ambiguity of feeling and makes us clear-headed partisans. Whether *Macbeth* goes on beyond this surmounting of melodramatic limitations to high achievement as tragedy is the final problem. It turns, I believe, on Shakespeare's treatment of Macbeth, that is, on whether this retains the complexity that cannot quite be replaced by the kind of complexities that *Macbeth* does embrace. Here, of course, we are in the area of our mode of response to character, where all is elusive and insecure, and we can only be speculative. What I have proposed, in general, is that, because of the manifold claims that Macbeth makes upon our sympathy, we are drawn into identification with him in his whole being; one might say that he tricks us into accepting more than we expect or realize. If it is true that we are led to experience empathy with a murderer and thus to come into a more complete 'feeling knowledge' of what human beings are like (tragic experience as the catharsis of self-ignorance), then Shakespeare has had a success which is not trivial. Yet there remains a legitimate question or two. Let us try this approach. It is not the business of tragedy to let man know that he is only a scoundrel or devil (any more than its business is to let him know that he is really an angel); it is obvious enough that such an experience would be too circumscribed to gain assent to its truthfulness. In so far as he pushes us in that direction, Shakespeare makes the indispensable qualifications. Yet the felt qualifications can be expressed in ways that are less than satisfactory; for instance, 'Macbeth is a villain, but there's also this to be said', or, still more, 'Macbeth is a wonderful man. Oh yes, a villain, of course.' Such flip statements are not found literally in *Macbeth* criticism, but they do represent the tendency to make a unitary assessment and then add an afterthought, that is, to pull the constituent elements apart unevenly instead of holding them together in a fusion not so simply describable.

It is possible that Shakespeare's basic method encourages this tendency. Shakespeare first chooses a protagonist who in action is worse than the other main tragic heroes, and then tends to make him better than other tragic heroes, in effect to make him now one, and now the other. Shakespeare had to protect Macbeth against the unmixed hostility that the mere villain would evoke; perhaps he over-protected him, letting him do all his villainies indeed, but providing him with an excess of devices for exciting the pity, warmth, and approval which prompt forgetfulness of the villainies. If critics have, as Knights protested, sentimentalized Macbeth, it may be that the text gives them more ground than has been supposed, that Shakespeare's own sympathy with Macbeth went beyond that which every artist owes to the evil man whom he wants to realize. We may be driven to concluding that Shakespeare has kept us at one with Macbeth, in whom the good man is all but annihilated by the tragic flaw, by making him the flawed man who is all but annihilated by the tragic goodness—that is, the singular appeal of the man trapped, disappointed, deserted, deprived of a wife, finished, but unwhimpering, contemplative, unyielding. If that is so, Shakespeare has kept us at one with a murderer by making him less than, or other than, a murderer.

This may seem a perverse conclusion after we have been pointing to the 'risks' Shakespeare took by showing Macbeth lengthily arranging the murder of Banquo and by having the murder of Lady Macduff and her children done partly on stage. The risk there, however, was of our separation from Macbeth as in melodrama; the risk here is of an empathic union on too easy grounds. For what is finally and extraordinarily spared Macbeth is the ultimate rigour of self-confrontation, the act of knowing directly what he has been and done. We see the world judging Macbeth, but not Macbeth judging himself. That consciousness of the nature of the deed which he has at the murder of Duncan gives way to other disturbances, and whatever sense of guilt, if any, may be inferred from his later distresses (we surveyed, early in section iii, the passages sometimes supposed to reveal a confessional or penitent strain), is far from an open facing and defining of the evil done—the murders, of course, the attendant lying, and, as is less often noted, the repeated bearing of false witness (II, iii, 99; III, i, 29 ff.; III, iv, 49). Of Cawdor, whose structural relationship to Macbeth is often mentioned, we are told that

> very frankly he confess'd his treasons,
> Implor'd your Highness' pardon, and set forth
> A deep repentance.

(I, iv, 5–7)

Macduff, with rather less on his conscience than Macbeth, could say,

> sinful Macduff,
> They were all struck for thee—nought that I am;
> Not for their own demerits, but for mine,
> Fell slaughter on their souls. (iv, iii, 224–7)

Cawdor and Macduff set the example which Macbeth never follows; or, to go outside the play, Othello and Lear set examples that Macbeth never follows. Part of Hamlet's agonizing is centred in his passion to avoid having to set such an example. Macbeth simply does not face the moral record. Instead he is the saddened and later bereaved husband, the man deprived of friends and future, the thinker, the pathetic believer in immunity, the fighter. These roles are a way of pushing the past aside—the past which cries out for a new sense, in him, of what it has been. If, then, our hypothesis about the nature of tragic participation is valid, the reader ends his life with and in Macbeth in a way that demands too little of him. He experiences forlornness and desolation, and even a kind of substitute triumph—anything but the soul's reckoning which is a severer trial than the world's judgment. He is not initiated into a true spaciousness of character, but follows, in Macbeth, the movement of what I have called a contracting personality. This is not the best that tragedy can offer.[19]

NOTES

1. See, for instance, Wolfgang J. Weilgart, 'Macbeth: Demon and Bourgeois', *Shakespeare Society of New Orleans Publications* (1946), and its citations, as well as the citations in Kenneth Muir's Introduction to the Arden *Macbeth* (1951 ff.), pp. xlviii ff. Weilgart's ill-written essay, based on Karl Jaspers's *Psychologie der Weltanschauungen* is not uninstructive.

2. For fuller quotations and appropriate comments, see Muir, *op. cit.* pp. lix ff. The Abercrombie quotation is from *The Idea of Great Poetry*, the Knight from *The Wheel of Fire* (Knight carried the idea further in *Christ and Nietzsche*, 1948).

3. *How Many Children Had Lady Macbeth?*, pp. 54–5.

4. Introduction to his edition of *Macbeth* (Boston, 1939), p. xiv.

5. George Clifford Rosser, Critical Commentary, *Macbeth* (1957), pp. 38, 39, 40, 44. This work might be compared with a Catholic schoolboy manual, the Rev. R. F. Walker's *Companion to the Study of Shakespeare: Macbeth* (1947). The often useful application of Catholic doctrine unfortunately keeps giving way to sermons.

6. William Allan Neilson and Charles Jarvis Hill (eds.), *The Complete Plays and Poems of Shakespeare* (Boston, 1942), p. 1183.

7. Cf. Gogol's *Inspector General*, where the meaning 'The way of transgressors is hard' is conveyed exclusively through characters acting in character.

8. *Op. cit.* p. lxxiv.

9. For convenience I shall use the word 'readers' to denote literal readers, spectators at the theatre, viewers, all those who see the play on stage or in print or in any other medium. I use 'we' to denote the hypothetical possessor of characteristic responsiveness.

10. Some critics always defend apparent authority; others redefine the character who has it; still others look for artistic signs that the apparent holder of authority has been subtly disavowed. Thus, one school accepts Gulliver's view of himself and of the Houyhnhnms; another argues that the total structure of Book IV turns the satire against Gulliver. The readers who accept Moll Flanders's view of things resort to various shifts to deal with her inconsistencies; the opposite way out is to treat Moll as a product of confusions in Defoe's own mind.

11. Even when an over-valuing of Brecht's theories puts something of a halo upon the *Verfremdungseffekt* and of a shadow upon *Einfühlung*. The inevitability of *Einfühlung*, whatever its precise character, is indicated by

Brecht's having to rewrite to try to prevent it after it had appeared in responses to his own work. Perhaps, however, we need a new term like 'consentience' to suggest more than 'sympathy' but less than 'identification' or 'empathy', which suffer from popular overuse.

12. *Shakespeare: The Great Tragedies*, Writers and Their Work No. 133 (1961), p. 35. Cf. his statement that 'the Poet for the Defence . . . can make us feel that we might have fallen in the same way' (Introduction, Arden edition, p. 1, and similarly on p. lvi).

13. Gorki's *Lower Depths*, Ibsen's *Wild Duck*, and O'Neill's *Iceman Cometh* are remarkably alike in their portrayal of the need of self-protective illusions; in effect they deny the possibility of the tragic experience of illumination. But recent playwrights like Osborne, Pinter, and Albee choose an opposite course: they make the reader identify with one evil or another by giving him nowhere else to go. They permit no illusions of saving virtue (though they may foster illusions of irremediable defectiveness). This is of course the way of satire, which aspires to much less than the tragic range of personality.

14. This difficulty will of course not exist for critics who believe that Macbeth, though a lost soul, has wrenched some sort of moral triumph from his career.

15. Muir's note on the passage (Arden edition, p. 165).

16. Among the accounts of Macbeth's descent one of the most interesting is that of W. C. Curry, *Shakespeare's Philosophical Patterns* (Baton Rouge, Louisiana, 1937).

17. Muir, *Shakespeare: The Great Tragedies*, p. 36. However, Muir uses the words rather incidentally to name one of the factors that may account for the difficulty of presenting the play successfully on the stage. He may not be strongly convinced that sympathies do switch. At any rate, his words conveniently summarize a point of view probably held widely.

18. Veronica Henriques, *The Face I Had* (1965), p. 38.

19. As Muir says, ' . . . the last two acts are not quite on the level of the first three' (*Shakespeare: The Great Tragedies*, p. 36). This is a passing comment, however, again in the context of the actability of the play. Cf. G. B. Harrison, ' . . . *Macbeth* is in some ways the least satisfactory of Shakespeare's mature tragedies. The last Act falls away . . .' This is from the Introduction to the Penguin *Macbeth* (1937), p. 17. But Harrison uses this statement to introduce the subject of revisions in the text.

Besides the comparisons that have been made, there is another that has elucidatory value. Garrick added to Macbeth's lines a closing speech which in content might have been inspired by the same sense of shortcoming that prevails in the present essay, but which is in the common rhetorical vein of eighteenth-century improvements of Shakespeare:

> Tis done! the scene of life will quickly close.
> Ambition's vain delusive dreams are fled,
> And now I wake to darkness, guilt, and horror;
> I cannot bear it! let me shake it off—
> It will not be; my soul is clog'd with blood—
> I cannot rise! I dare not ask for mercy—
> It is too late, hell drags me down; I sink,
> I sink,—my soul is lost for ever!—Oh!—Oh!

(Quoted in Arden edition, p. xlvi, n. 2.) One wonders whether Garrick was remembering Marlowe's *Dr Faustus*, which *Macbeth* resembles, notably in the great ambition of the hero, in the enormous struggle at the time of the first decisive step, and in the phenomena of psychic strain. Garrick's last four lines might be a précis of Faustus's final hundred lines. But this striking fact underscores the difference in the treatment of the two heroes: Faustus sees the whole truth of his career with utmost clarity, but because of a 'block', as we would say, cannot take advantage of the grace he rightly feels is offered; Macbeth, on the other hand, lacks this clarity and hence is hardly able to advance to the next stage, where the issue is spiritual despair.

IA Hell-castle as represented on the stage for the
Passion Play at Valenciennes, 1547

IB Christ Triumphant before the gate of Hell.
Oil painting by Giovanni Bellini, *c.* 1500

IC Hearne's print of
Christ's descent into
Hell

II Hell-castle as represented in the Doom, formerly in fresco on the church arch in the
Chapel of the Holy Cross, Stratford-upon-Avon

III Ellen Terry as Lady Macbeth, sketched by Sargent

IVA William Blake's *Pity*: a preliminary study

IVB William Blake's *Hecate*

V Macbeth in the witches' cave. Reproduced from
Rowe's edition, 1709

A Mrs Yates 'in Dollalolla's dress'

B David Garrick

C John Philip Kemble

D Charles and Ellen Kean

VI *Macbeth* costumes

VII Sarah Siddons as Lady Macbeth (I, v, 37–8).
Reproduced from a painting by George Henry Harlow

VIIIA Charles Kean's *Macbeth*. Princess's Theatre, 1853

VIIIB Beerbohm Tree's *Macbeth*. His Majesty's Theatre, 1911

IXA Sir Barry Jackson's *Macbeth*. Court Theatre, 1928

IXB *Macbeth*, Royal Shakespeare Theatre, 1962: directed by Donald McWhinnie,
setting by John Bury, costumes by Annena Stubbs. After the Banquet

X Edmund Kean as Macbeth (II, ii). Reproduced from
The Theatrical Inquisitor, November 1814

Mr MACKLIN,

In the Character of MACBETH.

Act II.d Scene 3.d

XI Macklin as Macbeth (II, iii). Reproduced from *The London Magazine*,
November 1773

XIIA Garrick and Mrs Pritchard in *Macbeth* (II, ii). Reproduced from
Green's mezzotint (1775) of a painting by Zoffany

XIIB Toshiro Mifune and Isuzu Yamada in Akira Kurosawa's film, *Throne of Blood*

XIII Henry Irving as Macbeth (I, iii). Reproduced from a photograph of a
drawing by Bernard Partridge, 29 December 1888

XIV *Macbeth*, Shakespeare Memorial Theatre, 1955: production by Glen Byam Shaw,
scenery and costumes by Roger Furse

XV Sybil Thorndike as Lady Macbeth (V, i). Reproduced from *The Sketch*, 5 January 1927

XVI Paul Scofield as Macbeth, Royal Shakespeare Theatre, 1967

HELL-CASTLE AND ITS DOOR-KEEPER

BY

GLYNNE WICKHAM

Few scenes in Shakespeare can have provoked more laughter in the theatre and more discomfort in the classroom than *Macbeth*, II, iii. At the centre of this paradox lies the character of the Porter, and in particular the obscenities which punctuate his remarks. These obscenities moreover are inextricably linked to a string of references to hell and the devil. How is this scene to be handled by the actor, and how is it to be handled by the schoolteacher?

The experience of being woken up in the middle of the night out of a deep sleep to deal with some disturbance in the house is as irritating as it is common: it is therefore a situation which if exposed to view in the theatre by a good mimic is certain to provide an amusing spectacle. Macbeth's porter, asleep when he ought to have been awake and on duty, stumbling towards the castle gate still rubbing his bleary eyes and hastily adjusting his costume, arouses a host of personal associations for everyone in the audience and is a sure-fire raiser of laughter in consequence. The fact that in this instance he is suffering from a bad hangover only adds to the fun for adults. Yet it is in this addition that trouble begins; for out of it spring the particular obscenities through which the Porter gives expression in his language both to his predicament and to his feelings. Normally speaking the teacher must reckon both this predicament and these feelings to lie outside the experience of schoolchildren; in consequence, no great effort of imagination is required to understand why many teachers (and some editors) should find themselves perplexed if not embarrassed when faced with the task of explaining this scene to their pupils. To take refuge in the old nostrums of a corrupt passage in the text or, more frequent, of 'comic relief', may ease the embarrassment, but shirks the challenge which the scene presents. Are the references to hell, the devil, drink and lechery to be regarded simply as a rag-bag of swear-words habitual to a coarse, unlettered peasant? Or are they pointers to the true significance of the scene and its function within the structure of the play?

I think it may be useful both to the actor and to the teacher to know that anyone familiar with medieval religious drama is likely to recognize a correspondence between the vocabulary of this scene and that of a similar playlet within the English Miracle Cycles, 'The Harrowing of Hell'. If this story has become unfamiliar, this is partly because it is an aspect of Christian belief which theologians of the Reformation distorted, and partly because modern Anglican opinion prefers to ignore it. Yet I think it is the story which provided Shakespeare with his model for the particular form in which he chose to cast Act II, scene iii of *Macbeth*, and possibly for the play as a whole.[1]

On the medieval stage hell was represented as a castle, more particularly as a dungeon or cesspit within a castle, one entrance to which was often depicted as a dragon's mouth (Plate IA). Its gate was guarded by a janitor or porter. Christ, after his crucifixion, but before his resurrection, came to this castle of hell to demand of Lucifer the release of the souls of the patriarchs and prophets. The setting for this play was either the interior of the gate-house or the courtyard of the castle: Christ's arrival was signalled by a tremendous knocking at this gate and a blast of trumpets. The gate eventually collapses allowing the Saviour-avenger, accompanied by the archangel Michael with his flaming sword, to enter and release the souls held prisoner within. It is in circumstances not unlike these that Macduff knocks at the gate of Macbeth's castle and that Malcolm and Donalbain escape from it in the course of Act II, scenes ii and iii. What did hell look like? How did its door-keeper behave? And where did the authors of the Miracle Cycles obtain descriptive information? The starting point may be found in two of the oldest mimetic ceremonies within the Catholic liturgy, the *Ordo Dedicationis Ecclesiae* and the *Tollite portas* procession to the city gates or church door on Palm Sunday, later elaborated and put to different use in the *Officium Elevationis Crucis*. Karl Young thinks that the inspiration of all these ceremonies is to be found in both the twenty-fourth Psalm, verses 7–10, and the second part of the 'Gospel of Nicodemus', the *Descensus Christi ad Inferos*.[2]

The first six and the last four verses of Psalm xxiv are virtually separate. It is the latter section which bears directly upon the two liturgical ceremonies.

7 Lift up your heads, O ye gates, and be ye lift up, ye everlasting doors : and the King of glory shall come in.

8. Who is the King of glory : it is the Lord strong and mighty, even the Lord mighty in battle.

9 Lift up your heads, O ye gates, and be ye lift up, ye everlasting doors : and the King of glory shall come in.

10 Who is the King of glory : even the Lord of hosts, he is the King of glory.

(Book of Common Prayer)

These words appear in the Latin text of the *Descensus* but as a duologue between Christ and Satan. This dialogue is brought to life in emblematic manner within the *Ordo Dedicationis Ecclesiae*.

A church before consecration was regarded as impure, the dwelling place of Satan and in need of cleansing. Accordingly the bishop approached the building in procession on Christ's behalf, knocked at the West door with his staff three times and said in Latin,

Tollite portas, principes, vestras, et elevamini, portae aeternales, et introibit rex gloriae.

A cleric replies from within the building,

Quis est iste rex gloriae?

This dialogue is repeated three times after which the bishop declares,

Dominus virtutum, ipse est rex gloriae.

As he enters the church the cleric slips out. The church itself is then cleansed by censing. This ceremony can be traced back to the fourth century in Jerusalem.[3]

A full account of the symbolic representation of the Harrowing of Hell derived from the *Elevatio* survives in England from the monastery of Barking, near London. Katherine of Sutton, abbess of Barking from 1363 to 1376, established a ceremony there incorporating the *Tollite portas* verses and lying immediately between the close of Matins on Easter Day and the normal *Visitatio Sepulchri*. At Barking, members of the convent were imprisoned within the Chapel of St Mary Magdalen, thus representing the souls of the patriarchs confined in hell. A priest approaches the door with the words *Tollite portas*; the door is opened and the erstwhile prisoners file out into the church carrying palm branches signifying victory over Satan and death, singing *Cum rex gloriae*. This ceremony also survives from Dublin in two forms.[4]

The authors of the vernacular cycles therefore had a long liturgical tradition behind them as well as the Gospel of Nicodemus to assist them when they came to prepare their play-books of the Harrowing of Hell. The story itself was familiar enough to require little development: ample opportunity existed, however, for the addition of descriptive detail. In this the authors were further assisted by artists in stained glass and by painters who, from Fra Angelico to Bellini and Dürer, had persistently represented Christ with the banner of the cross in his hand standing victorious, like St George above the dragon, before the shattered gates of hell with Satan cringing at his feet (Plate IB).

In *Macbeth*, Macduff enters Macbeth's castle twice, first in II, iii, when Duncan's murder is discovered and Malcolm and Donalbain escape, and again in v, ix, when, as a victorious general, he arrives from the field of battle and addresses Malcolm:

> Hail, King! for so thou art. Behold, where stands
> Th' usurper's cursed head: the time is free.[5] (v, ix, 20–1)

There is thus no attempt on Shakespeare's part to provide a direct parallel to the Harrowing of Hell within the play of *Macbeth*; but there is ample evidence within the text of the play of a conscious attempt on Shakespeare's part to remind his audience of this ancient and familiar story so that they may discern for themselves the moral meaning of this stage narrative abstracted from the annals of Scottish history. To make this point as forcibly as I think it should be made it is first necessary to reconstruct from the texts and stage directions of the surviving Miracle Cycles the picture of hell and its inhabitants that was familiar to Tudor audiences together with the salient aspects of the story as it was treated on their stages.

Hell itself was represented as a combination of castle, dungeon and cesspit. Of the four surviving English Cycles, Towneley (Play xxv), 'The Deliverance of Souls', follows York (Play 37), The Saddlers, almost verbatim at times: both are derived in large measure from the Middle-English poetical 'Gospel of Nicodemus' of the early fourteenth century.[6] It is from these versions of the play that we learn that hell is equipped with walls and gates like a castle.

TOWNELEY:

> *Belzabub.* Go, spar the yates, yH mot thou the!
> And set the waches on the waH. (E.E.T.S. lines 120–1)

YORK:

> *Bellial.* We! spere oure ӡates, all ill mot þou spede,
> And sette furthe watches on þe wall.
> (L. Toulmin-Smith, *York Plays* (1885), p. 380, lines 139–40)

This image of Hell-castle is later reinforced in Towneley (lines 146–9) by Belzabub who calls to Satan

> *Belzabub.* Thou must com help to spar
> we are beseged abowte.
> *Sathanas.* Besegyd aboute! whi, who durst be so bold
> for drede to make on us a fray?

41

In the *Ludus Coventriae* Anima Christi describes hell as 'the logge (*prison*) of helle' (E.E.T.S. p. 305). This is followed by a stage direction which reads: 'The soule goth to helle gatys . . .' which gates Christ further specifies as being a 'derke dore' (*ibid.* p. 306). This image of a prison is consistently maintained in the plays of 'The Fall of Lucifer' and the 'The Assumption' from the same Cycle and is further particularized by Belial (p. 319) as 'helle gonge', i.e. latrine. In the Towneley 'Deliverance' hell is also described as a 'pryson' (by Jesus, line 236) and as 'that pytt' (by Jesus, line 285) and as 'hell pyt' (by Satan, line 360). Prison, pit and dungeon are the words used variously in the Chester cycle to describe hell (Plate II).

What we must visualize is an edifice which, viewed from outside, resembles a castle and, viewed from inside, a sequence of dark dungeons and torture chambers pervaded by stench and heat. This picture, built up from details in the texts of English cyclic plays set in hell, closely resembles the MS. picture of Hell-castle illustrating the Valenciennes Passion Play of 1547 (see Plate I A). Further detail, if we want it, can be found in the Account Book of the Mons Passion Play (1501) where the walls of hell are said to have been 'plastered'.[7] A Scottish castle therefore, through the gates of which a kingly guest has been welcomed by a host who promptly murders him, might be calculated to recall this other, satanic castle with its 'ʒatys of sorwatorie (*torment*)'.[8] Both castles moreover are equipped with a janitor or porter.

The authors of the Cycles found this door-keeper in the poetical 'Gospel of Nicodemus' where, as a character, he already borders on the comic.

> *Dominus.* Wer ys nou þis ʒateward?
> me þuncheþ [*thinketh*] he is a coward.
> *Janitor.* Ich haue herd wordes stronge,
> ne dar y her no lengore stonde;
> kepe þe gates whose may,
> y lete hem stonde ant renne away.[9]

This idea is elaborated upon by the York and Towneley scribes. In both plays the porter acquires a name; significantly it is Rybald, a word defined by *O.E.D.* as meaning 'Scurrilous, irreverent, profane, indecent' and as derived from the French *ribaut*, a menial. A more succinct and apposite description of Macbeth's porter could scarcely be found. In the Towneley play Rybald receives his orders from Belzabub. In *Macbeth*, the Porter's first question is,

> Who's there, i' th' name of Belzebub?   (line 4)

We should surely expect him to say 'in the name of my master' or possibly 'in the name of Macbeth'; but, since Macbeth has just murdered Duncan, 'in the name of Belzebub' or 'in the devil's name' is just as appropriate. The knocking has at least put the porter in mind of Hell-gate: his comments put it in our minds too. In the Towneley 'Deliverance' it is Rybald who first answers Christ's knocking.

> *Rybald.* . . . what deviłł is he
> That callys hym kyng over us ałł?
> hark belzabub, com ne,
> ffor hedusly I hard hym całł.   (E.E.T.S. lines 116–19)

The 'hideous call' is a fanfare of trumpets followed by the familiar,

Attollite portas, principes, vestras & eleuamini porte eternales, & introibit rex glorie. (Towneley, lines 115–16)

At York and Chester the Latin is followed by a translation, phrase by phrase, into English.

In *Macbeth* the Porter receives no answer to his thrice-repeated 'Who's there?' The knocking continues remorselessly, but the questions are answered rhetorically by the Porter himself. In his drunken condition he stumbles about the stage like a man waking out of a dream who still regards the environment of his dream as more real than that confronting him on waking. Just, as today, one might be woken by one's own telephone and at the same time fancy oneself called to some other 'phone in another house within the fabric of one's dream, so the Porter, dreaming that he is Rybald and in hell, associates the real knocking on Macbeth's castle-gate that has obtruded upon or into his dream with Christ's arrival at hell's 'dark door'. When the Porter asks for the first time who is knocking he is still firmly in his dream-world.

Who's there, i' th' name of Belzebub?　　　　　　(line 4)

When he asks for the second time he is already beginning to slip out of his dream, for he can't recall the name of any other companion in this diablerie.

Who's there, i' th' other devil's name?　　　　　　(line 8)

By the time he has repeated this question a third time the chill of dawn is bringing him swiftly back to reality.

—But this place is too cold for Hell.
I'll devil-porter it no further:　　　　　　(lines 18–19)

This gate is not shattered: the porter opens it. Macduff enters. The porter asks for a tip.

I pray you, remember the porter.　　　　　　(line 22)

This remark is ambivalent, for it can be addressed by the actor both to Macduff and to the audience. As in the Porter's dream, it is in two worlds at once; that of Macbeth's castle and that of another scene from another play which has just been recalled for the audience and which the author wants them to remember. If we take the remark in this latter sense, we recollect that it was Jesus who with a loud knocking entered Hell-castle in search of Satan. At this point in *Macbeth* Shakespeare has not yet informed us that Macduff is destined to avenge Duncan's murder, but in his use of the porter he gives us a clear hint of what to expect.

In the next sixteen lines of conversation with Macduff, the porter sobers up and drops every aspect of his earlier hallucination; but in the ribaldry of the language, humour and (where the actor is concerned) gesture, he remains equivocal. When Macduff asks him,

Is thy master stirring?　　　　　　(line 43)

we are still at liberty to regard him both as Macbeth's servant and as Satan's.

It is then left to Lennox who has entered the castle with Macduff to draw the audience's attention to another strange phenomenon.

> *Lennox.* The night has been unruly: where we lay,
> Our chimneys were blown down; and as they say,
> Lamentings heard i' th' air; strange screams of death,
> And, prophesying with accents terrible,

43

Of dire combustion, and confus'd events,
New hatch'd to th' woeful time, the obscure bird
Clamour'd the livelong night: some say the earth
Was feverous, and did shake.
        Macbeth.   'Twas a rough night.
        Lennox. My young remembrance cannot parallel
A fellow to it.   (lines 55–63)

An older memory, however, might well recall a parallel. In the cyclic plays of the Harrowing of Hell it is the strange noises in the air which alert the devils of impending disaster.

TOWNELEY

Rybald. Sen fyrst that hell was mayde / And I was put therin, / Sich sorow neuer ere I had / nor hard I sich a dyn; /

· · · · · · · · ·

how, belsabub! bynde thise boys, / sich harow was neuer hard in hell.
        Belzabub. Out, rybald! thou rores, / what is betyd? can thou oght tell?
        Rybald. Whi, herys thou not this ugly noyse?   (lines 89–95)

When Christ arrives at the gates there is more noise including trumpets and knocking.

CHESTER (stage direction)

Tunc veniet Jhesus et fiet Clamor vel sonitus materialis magnus . . .   (line 144)

Still more succinct is the stage direction of the Mons Passion:

Lors se doi(b)t faire en En(f)fer une grande tempeste et la terre doit trambler.   (ed. cit. p. 412)

Lennox might be supplying a literal translation of this last line with his 'some say the earth was feverous and did shake'.[10]

It is Lady Macbeth who completes the picture. It was she who first heard the knocking at the south gate from the direction of England and it is she who, when the bell starts tolling, says,

                   What's the business,
        That such a hideous trumpet calls to parley
        The sleepers of the house?   (lines 81–3)

It was Rybald in the Towneley 'Deliverance' who cried out to Beelzebub on hearing Christ's trumpets at Hell-gate
                              . . . come ne,
        ffor hedusly I hard hym call.   (lines 118–19) (Plate I c)

Thunder, cacophony, screams and groans were the audible emblems of Lucifer and hell on the medieval stage. Those same aural emblems colour the whole of II, iii of *Macbeth* and, juxtaposed as they are with thunderous knocking at a gate attended by a porter deluded into regarding himself as a devil, their relevance to the moral meaning of the play could scarcely have escaped the notice of its first audiences.

In the cyclic plays of the Harrowing of Hell, Satan (or Lucifer) is physically overthrown, bound and either cast into hell pit or sinks into it.

CHESTER (stage direction) Iaceant tunc Sathanam de sede sua. (line 168)

TOWNELEY:

> *Sathan.* Alas, for doyll and care!
> I synk into hell pyt. (lines 359–60)

In the York play the rescued souls leave the stage singing *Laus tibi Domino cum gloria*. Towneley ends with the *Te Deum*. In *Macbeth*, when Macduff has successfully brought Macbeth and his 'fiend-like Queen' to justice, it is Malcolm, the new King-elect, who brings the play to its close in joy and thanksgiving.

> *Malcolm.* So thanks to all at once, and to each one,
> Whom we invite to see us crown'd at Scone. *Flourish. Exeunt.* (v, ix, 140–1)

Scotland has been purged of a devil who, like Lucifer, aspired to a throne that was not his, committed crime upon crime first to obtain it and then to keep it, and was finally crushed within the refuge of his own castle by a saviour-avenger accompanied by armed archangels. Hell has been harrowed: 'the time is free'.

© G. WICKHAM 1966

NOTES

1. John W. Hales in his *Notes and Essays on Shakespeare* (1884) regarded the Porter as a possible borrowing from the English Miracle Cycles (pp. 284–6). He appears only to have been familiar with *Ludus Coventriae*, the one cycle of the four in which Belzebub is not a character of importance in 'The Descent into Hell'; but he also draws attention to the porter of hell gate as depicted by Heywood in *Four P's* and in the much later anonymous Interlude *Nice Wanton*: see also William Hone, *Ancient Mysteries Described* (1823), pp. 120–47.

This suggestion does not appear to have been carried much further until John B. Harcourt raised it again in 'I Pray You, Remember the Porter', *Shakespeare Quarterly*, XII (1961), 393–402. This important article, which was brought to my attention after the completion of this short essay, anticipates several of the points made in it and draws attention to several other significant details in the scene. The fact that the two articles were written independently of each other and in different continents perhaps serves to strengthen the more important conclusions that are common to them both.

2. *The Drama of the Medieval Church* (1933), I, 149 ff. See also *The Middle English Harrowing of Hell and Gospel of Nicodemus*, ed. W. H. Hulme for E.E.T.S. (1907), pp. lxii ff.

3. Young, *op. cit.* I, 102.

4. *Ibid.* pp. 168 ff.

5. This and other quotations from *Macbeth* are from the Arden edition.

6. See W. H. Hulme, *op. cit.* pp. xviii ff.

7. See G. Cohen, *Le Livre de Conduite du Régisseur et le Compte des Dépenses pour le Mystère de la Passion joué à Mons en 1501* (Paris, 1925), pp. 498, 528.

8. *Ludus Coventriae* (E.E.T.S.), p. 306.

9. Harley MS. Text L, *The Harrowing of Hell*, ed. cit. p. 13, lines 139–44.

10. These extraordinary noises are clearly intended to be associated as much with the murder of Duncan as with the arrival of Macduff and are derived as clearly from the noises associated with the actual moment of Christ's death as from noise associated with the arrival of Anima Christi before the gates of hell. The Harley Text of the *Gospel of Nicodemus* describing this moment reads:

> þe stanes in sonder brak,
> þe erth trembled & quaked,
> with noys als man it spak,
> Slyke mane for him it maked.

(Hulme, *op. cit.* for E.E.T.S., p. 68, lines 705–8)

Additional note. John Heywood in *The Play Called the Four PP* (ll. 819–48) refers to the Porter of Hell Gate in the Corpus Christi play presented at Coventry, where Shakespeare may have seen it before its final production in 1581.

45

'HIS FIEND-LIKE QUEEN'

BY

W. MOELWYN MERCHANT

It is surely unnecessary to argue today that Lady Macbeth's invocation of the 'spirits that tend on mortal thoughts', of the 'murth'ring ministers', is a formal stage in demonic possession—though the implications of that statement are rarely if ever pursued. W. C. Curry sufficiently stated[1] the spiritual significance of the invocation in saying that 'Lady Macbeth deliberately wills that [unclean spirits, wicked angels] subtly invade her body and so control it that the natural inclination of the spirit towards goodness and compassion may be completely extirpated'. But even this statement we may regard as slightly evasive and carrying some of the tones of Coleridge's examination of her character:

Hers is the mock fortitude of a mind deluded by ambition; she shames her husband with a superhuman audacity of fancy which she cannot support . . . Her speech: 'Come, all you spirits that tend on mortal thoughts,' etc., is that of one who had habitually familiarised her imagination to dreadful conceptions, and was trying to do so still more. Her invocations and requisitions are all the false efforts of a mind accustomed only hitherto to the shadows of imagination . . .

'Fancy which she cannot support . . . trying to do so . . . false efforts', these qualified phrases do less than justice to the force of the invocation at I, v, 40–54; it denies the position which Lady Macbeth holds in the supernatural pattern of the play, her relations to the Weird Sisters and to Hecate; it minimizes the poetic and dramatic organization of scenes iii–vii of Act I.

We should not, perhaps, be surprised that the impact of the demonic invocation is reduced, both in critical reading and in our experience in the theatre. For our emotional attention is deflected, while our immediate understanding is reduced by inadequate attention to the technical force of some of the phrases. In the first place we experience a sharp sexual affront to our sensibility in the two phrases 'unsex me here' and 'come to my woman's breasts,/And take my milk for gall' and it is not insignificant, in weighing this sense of affront, that two classical performances in the role sprang from a conception of great and essentially feminine beauty: Sarah Siddons conceived Lady Macbeth as possessing 'all the subjugating powers of intellect and all the charms and graces of personal beauty . . . that character which I believe is generally allowed to be most captivating to the other sex,—fair, feminine, nay, perhaps even fragile'; while Sargent's swift *grisaille* sketch of Ellen Terry in the National Portrait Gallery establishes a like impression of grace and of spontaneity (Plate III). Unless, therefore, Lady Macbeth as 'fiend-like queen' is played in a naïvely 'monumental' way, the demand that her sex be destroyed carries a shocking force.

But in fact the sexual affront is profounder than this immediate experience in performance and relates this scene intimately to its context in the first act. The scene itself (I, v) is close-knit. It opens with Macbeth's letter, ambiguous, allusive, technical: 'they' are as undefined, questionable, as they were in I, i and I, iii; on the other hand a precise phrase, 'they made themselves air', a known power of witchcraft to create a distinct, almost palpable atmosphere into which the

46

initiate may vanish, places and defines their expertise; the pun on 'mortal knowledge' (both 'human' and 'death-dealing') anticipates the 'mortal thoughts' of Lady Macbeth's soliloquy; while the complicity, the intimacy in evil of the two protagonists, is left undefined and unfocused. With the opening of Lady Macbeth's comment on the letter we are referred back to Macbeth's last speech in the previous scene: her grouped antitheses—'Thou wouldst be great . . . but without the illness', 'wouldst not play false,/And yet', 'Rather thou dost fear . . . than wishest should be undone'—precisely echo the thought and grammatical construction of his speech (reflecting an embarrassed dislocation in moral judgment):

> Let not light see my black and deep desires.
> The eye wink at the hand; *yet* let that be,
> Which the eye fears, when it is done, to see.

The ambiguity of her present status and power is extended in the 'spirits' which she would pour into his ear; while the near contempt of her phrase 'the milk of human kindness', that maternal source of compassion, prepares for her own 'unsexing'. The invocation itself proceeds in a formal ritual of demonic possession. The opening lines, in which the entry of the spirits shall unsex her, reflect both the uncertain nature of the Weird Sisters' (I, iii, 45, 'you should be women,/And yet your beards . . .') and the ambiguous rites of witchcraft which may be directed either to fertility or sterility, as we shall see; the transmutation for which she prays, making thick her blood, frustrating remorse and compunction, moves from bodily possession to moral confusion in which purpose and act, will and fulfilment, are disjointed and without 'peace'; finally, in two concluding invocations, 'Come to my woman's breasts', 'Come, thick Night', the moment of demonic possession is given its proper context, palled 'in the dunnest smoke of hell'.

Closer attention is demanded by the phrase, 'take my milk for gall', which has been a continuous editorial problem. From Samuel Johnson to our own day, a favoured solution has been to assume that Lady Macbeth desires simply that the 'murth'ring ministers' 'take away my milk, and put gall into the place', Johnson's paraphrase which Kenneth Muir endorses as 'the best' in his opinion. But this is to mitigate the supernatural force of the whole passage and it is unfortunate that Keightley's tentative solution[2] was not pursued to a proper conclusion: 'Perhaps we should read *with* for "for", taking "take" in the sense of *tinge, infect*, a sense it often bears.' We may deduce from this unnecessary emendation of '*for* gall' that Keightley appears to suppose a wholly physical tainting of the milk with the savour of gall. Had he pressed the 'sense it often bears' further than editors have ventured, he would have reached the wholly acceptable technical interpretation of the phrase, 'bewitch my milk for gall, possess it and complete the invasion of my body at its source of compassion'. There is ample confirmation for this reading and adequate parallels in Shakespeare, fully noted in the glossaries and lexicons. Robert Nares[3] explains the verb:

In the sense of to blast; or to affect violently, as by witchcraft. Sh. says of Herne, the hunter, that

> There he blasts the tree, and takes the cattle,
> And makes milch kine yield blood

and cites Gervase Markham's explanation of 'a horse that is taken',

Some farriers, not well understanding the ground of the disease, conster the word *taken* to be striken by some planet or evil spirit.

C. T. Onions cites the fullest passage (*Hamlet*, I, i, 163) in the sense 'to strike with disease':

> No spirit dares stir abroad,
> The nights are wholesome; then no planets strike,
> No fairy *takes*, nor witch hath power to charm,

while in the two instances from *Lear* (III, iv, 60 and II, iv, 166) Onions glosses the word as 'blasting, malignant influence' and 'blasting, pernicious' ('bless thee from whirlwinds, star-blasting and taking' and 'strike her young bones,/You taking airs, with lameness'). It is of course clear that these instances have in common a sense of cosmic disruption, supernatural evil and the infection of the body by planetary or demonic influences. In the last passage cited, Lear's cursing of Regan (as he had earlier disowned Cordelia by the 'mysteries of Hecate and the night') concludes with terms which recall *Macbeth*: '*Infect* her beauty . . . *blast* her pride.'

That Lady Macbeth, therefore, should consummate the possession of her body by this technical term, 'take my milk for gall',[4] completes the significance of this complex passage. That she should have deplored the natural, instinctively humane impulses of Macbeth a little earlier in the terms, 'too full o' th' milk of human kindness', is of a piece with this disruption of her nature; in the light of this closer examination of her words, the question put with irony by L. C. Knights, 'How many children had Lady Macbeth?', takes on more critical significance. The organic relationship, moreover, between this scene and those on either side (I, iii–vii) can now be more closely established. They deserve more detailed examination than can be given here but two related themes may be taken to make the connexion, that of judgment and justice, and of ministering servants.

Lady Macbeth has presumed to judge her husband, reversing the customary moral categories and taking his humane scrupulosity as merely ineffectual weakness. That this has in fact an element of truth in no way diminishes her moral obliquity in passing judgment. She, in the process of judging him, commits herself, her body and her spiritual functions to a Faustian service; nor is it, in this instance either, any diminution of her moral responsibility that her submission to demonic powers should condemn her in the rest of the play to a merely passive damnation. Macbeth's spiritual degeneration in this first act is both subtler and more scrupulous (and we do not forget here that scrupulosity can be a moral failing as well as a virtue). For Macbeth is involved, from his first contact with the Weird Sisters, in a self-examination dependent on the terminology of divine and human justice. The process begins with his first soliloquy (I, iii, 127–42). The lines,

> This supernatural soliciting
> Cannot be ill; cannot be good

may be felt to have 'the sickening see-saw rhythm' which L. C. Knights finds, confirming the quality of a 'phantasma, or a hideous dream'; it certainly has more profoundly an exploration, in rhetorical, antithetic form, of the status of the Weird Sisters' prophecy. The deep horror of the passage lies in the rational structure—'If ill . . . if good, why . . . ?'—within which the moral problem is explored, united to a mounting emotional tension. The lines from 'Present fears' to 'what is not' are an almost syllogistic conclusion to a moral argument but carrying for the attentive reader, in the final lines,

> That function is smother'd in surmise,
> And nothing is but what is not,

an anticipation of Macbeth's ultimate nullity, his conviction that life is a 'tale told by an idiot ... signifying nothing'. Yet the moment of rationalized horror in I, iii leads not to emotional disintegration but to Macbeth's total intellectual control in his response to Banquo at the end of the scene:

> Think upon what hath chanc'd; and at more time,
> *The interim having weigh'd it*, let us speak—

concerning which Steevens has the wholly just comment: the 'intervening portion' of time is personified: it (the 'Interim') is represented as 'a cool impartial judge' and so is Macbeth, having conquered his first revulsion from the 'supernatural soliciting'.[5]

Lady Macbeth, her compact with the 'murth'ring ministers' made firm, employs terms of judgment with fewer scruples than her husband. In response to Duncan's 'We are your guest tonight' (I, vi, 25) she replies in the terminology of judicial process:

> Your servants ever
> Have theirs, themselves, and what is theirs, in *compt*,
> To *make their audit* at your Highness' pleasure,

(terms regularly used both for human justice and for the Last Judgment).[6] Five lines later, at the opening of scene vii, Macbeth returns to his theme of judgment in its most elaborate form. If Roy Walker[7] is correct in his conjecture that "t were well/It were done quickly' and 'chalice' recall the Last Supper and Christ's words to Judas concerning His betrayal—'that thou doest, do quickly'—then supernatural, 'even-handed Justice' has here its profoundest analogy. The contrast could scarcely be pointed more strongly between Lady Macbeth's total submission to her course, with a casual acceptance of the terms of justice between herself and her royal guest, and Macbeth's extended casuistic examination of the relationship of 'double trust' in which he and Duncan stand within the context of eternal justice.

A similar contrast in the use of identical terminology may be seen in the image of 'servants' and 'attendant ministers' which also links these scenes. It begins at Macbeth's personification of his duties to his royal master as 'children and servants' 'Which do but what they should, by doing everything' (I, iv, 26), related to Christ's 'unprofitable servants' in St Luke xvii, 10, who do no more than their duty in doing all. The image is intensified and transferred from the gracious to the demonic in Lady Macbeth's 'Spirits that *tend* on mortal thoughts' and the ministers of sightless substance who '*wait* on Nature's mischief'. These verbs, *tend* and *wait*, applied to evil spirits or angels inevitably recall the biblical terminology of angelic attendance, 'waiting upon God'.[8] The contrast is made most intense in scene vii, after Macbeth's examination of his relation to Duncan as host, kinsman and subject; not only has Duncan these formal, social claims on Macbeth's integrity; 'his virtues will plead like angels, trumpet-tongu'd', in the final phrase uniting the angels of the Last Judgment with those 'who stand and wait' at the throne of God.

At this point in our examination of the dramatic contrast between Macbeth and his wife and their involvement in both good and evil supernature, we may profitably look to other sources of insight into Shakespeare's imagery. Blake clearly considered that the matter of two of his 'colour prints', *Pity* and *Hecate* (both derived in content substantially from *Macbeth*), were intimately related together. They are similar in size (*c.* 17 in. × 21 in. and *c.* 17 in. × 23 in.); they have consistently belonged together since they went first into the collection of Blake's friend Thomas Butts (they are now in the Tate Gallery, with versions elsewhere; Plates IV A, B), and Martin Butlin notes[9] their close identity of theme, for *Hecate* 'is probably a companion print to *Pity* . . . The two subjects were probably chosen to show two aspects of woman in the Fall. The triple representation of the Infernal Goddess Hecate is a traditional symbol of the three phases of the moon, crescent, full and waning.' The Weird Sisters number among the contents of their cauldron 'slips of yew,/Sliver'd in the moon's eclipse', a poisonous ingredient of which K. M. Briggs has extended the significance for this play. For yew is a 'tree of death' while 'Black magic is the magic of sterility; the moon's waxing time has always been counted the time of growth, and the moon's eclipse therefore would be the time of complete negation'.[10] Hecate is of course frequently (in her 'waxing time') associated with fertility,[11] but the associations in this play (and consistently in all Shakespeare's references to her elsewhere) are with destruction, sterility and death. Lady Macbeth's invocation of a demonism which denies her natural sex matches Macbeth's conviction of evil as he prepares (I, i, 50 ff.) for Duncan's murder:

> Nature seems dead, and wicked dreams abuse
> The curtain'd sleep: Witchcraft celebrates
> Pale Hecate's offerings; and wither'd Murther . . .
> Moves like a ghost.

Macbeth's second reference to Hecate is also involved with murder; as he obscurely hints at Banquo's death he sets its atmosphere and accompaniment—the activity of a witch's familiars and of Hecate:

> Ere the bat hath flown
> His cloister'd flight; ere to black Hecate's summons
> The shard-born beetle with his drowsy hums
> Hath rung night's yawning peal.

Blake's brooding, curiously noble figure of Hecate with her court of familiars very adequately depicts 'the goddess of hell and of sorcery', in whose name Lear disclaims all paternal care in Cordelia, by 'The mysteries of Hecate and the night' (I, i, 112); under whose influence the Player King in *Hamlet* is murdered, by a

> Mixture rank, of midnight weeds collected,
> With Hecat's ban thrice blasted, thrice infected—

and who is the appropriate term of abuse for Joan, la Pucelle, 'that railing Hecate' (*1 Henry VI*, III, ii, 64). We do not, then, require Hecate's presence on the stage to establish her presiding power over those in *Macbeth* who owe the same allegiance which Puck acknowledges; the number of those

that do run
By the triple Hecate's team
From the presence of the sun,
Following darkness like a dream.

This is the demonic company to which Lady Macbeth has committed herself and to which his increasing bloodshed drives Macbeth.

Before this submission to the triple Hecate's force, however, Macbeth, in contemplating his first murder, has a more daunting because more gracious vision; if Duncan's virtues will themselves be trumpeting angels, invoking final judgment against his 'taking-off', 'Pity' will declare his guilt more widely:

Shall blow the horrid deed in every eye,
That tears shall drown the wind.

Here we have yet another antithesis in the relation of Macbeth and his 'fiend-like queen'. Her allegiance is to 'mortal' powers who may ultimately hold of Hecate; Macbeth's awareness of submission to 'black Hecate's summons' is of slower growth and interrupted by knowledge of the other supernatural realm of grace. Blake's *Pity*, it is true, is involved in his own private mythology of the Fall but it nonetheless faithfully records the images of Macbeth's vision. The presiding image is that of Psalm xviii (in Coverdale's version):

He rode upon the Cherubyns and did flye; he came flyenge with the winges of the wynde.

Blake conflates the image of the Cherubins who fly *upon* the wind (the female figures, one of whom takes up the naked child) with the 'sightless couriers', the latter word a literal translation of 'angel'. Into this swift motion of grace 'pity' is swept up, the innocent helplessness of the phrase 'naked new-born babe' acquiring power ('striding the blast') from the mounted 'Cherubins'. The relation between Blake's print and Macbeth's speech merits more extended analysis but this would interpret Blake rather than Shakespeare. It suffices at this moment to focus the conflict, which as late as I, vii distinguishes the tugging of sin and grace in Macbeth from the swift demonism of Lady Macbeth. This struggle moreover establishes sharply the superior gravity of Shakespeare's treatment of evil supernature from that of all his contemporaries including King James.[12]

To summarize the argument: Lady Macbeth's willed submission to demonic powers, her unequivocal resolve to lay her being open to the invasion of witchcraft, is held in dramatic contrast to the painful, casuistic deliberations of Macbeth. She takes her appropriate dramatic place in the company of those, on the one hand, whose supernatural status is obscure; are the Weird Sisters witches, norns, fates or hallucinations? Holinshed expressed the historic doubts:

But afterwards the common opinion was, that these women were either the weird sisters, that is (as ye would say) the goddesses of destinie, or else some nymphs or feiries, indued with knowledge of prophesie by their necromanticall science.

Whatever the ambiguity of their status, we have, on the other hand, no doubt of Hecate's significance in Shakespeare's exploration of the supernatural; nor have we doubt (we see the

51

evidence on stage) of the 'necromantic' desires of Lady Macbeth; we see her bequeath her soul to demonic powers as irrevocably as Faustus. For Hecate broods over this play, whatever the status of the 'interpolated scenes'. The Weird Sisters owe her direct allegiance; Macbeth and Lady Macbeth submit themselves to a less mythical order of damnation, but even in their vision of hell Hecate and her followers belong as of right.

© W. M. MERCHANT 1966

NOTES

1. *Shakespeare's Philosophical Patterns* (Louisiana University Press, 1937).

2. *The Shakespeare Expositor* (1867); cited Furness *in loc.*

3. *A Shakespeare Glossary* (1901 ed., revised and enlarged by Halliwell and Wright).

4. I am grateful to Professor and Mrs Alan Ross (Birmingham) for confirming my conjecture in the following terms:
Take in the sense 'bewitch' presents no difficulties; it is *OED: Take* v. 7a and cf. *Take* sb. 3. The suggested translative use of *for* is perhaps more difficult: can *for* in fact mean 'so as to become'? It seems that it can; this sense is effectively *OED: For, prep, and conj.* A 8b, as used in *to go for a soldier*, that is, 'to go so as to become a soldier'.

5. Milton uses the word in the same sense, when Eve is first tempted by the fruit which 'Sollicited her longing eye'.

6. For *account* (*compt*) and *audit* as metaphors for the process of judgment, and more particularly the Last Judgment, cf. Romans XIV, 12: 'Every one of us shall give account of himself to God', and analogous passages which involve the concept of stewardship.

7. Cited by Muir *in loc.*

8. Cf. Revelation VIII, 2: 'And I saw the seven angels which stood before God; and to them were given seven trumpets.'

9. *William Blake*, Tate Gallery Catalogue, 1957, p. 43. Cf. also W. M. Merchant, 'Blake's Shakespeare', *Apollo*, Shakespeare Centenary Issue (April 1964); and Merchant, *Shakespeare and the Artist* (1959), ch. 10.

10. K. M. Briggs, *Pale Hecate's Team* (1962), p. 80.

11. Hecate is not only complex in herself as Triple-goddess (or on occasion quadruple); she varies greatly in significance. As a lunar goddess she was associated with fertility but in literary reference she was more frequently destructive. Elizabethans would be familiar with the passage in Ovid, *Metamorphoses*, XIV, 403–5:

> Illa nocens spargit virus sucosque veneni
> et Noctem Noctisque deos Ereboque Chaoque
> convocat et longis Hecaten ululatibus orat;

which was translated rather vaguely by Golding with no direct reference to Hecate. In *Comus* she was a destructive goddess of riot.

12. This 'gravity' in no way assumes Shakespeare's assent to contemporary attitudes. It does however mark the gulf between Shakespeare's tone and that of the writers available to him. The ephemera and the contemporary accounts of witch trials are for the most part merely credulous and marked by an unpleasant 'curiositas'; works of the authority of *Demonologie* have more sobriety but lean heavily on traditional classics such as the *Malleus Maleficorum*. Shakespeare's dramatic tone is both serious and exploratory.

THE FIEND-LIKE QUEEN:
A NOTE ON *MACBETH* AND SENECA'S
MEDEA

BY

INGA-STINA EWBANK

Not everyone is, perhaps, prepared to say that '*Macbeth* without Seneca would have been impossible';[1] but many would agree with Henry N. Paul when he calls *Macbeth* 'the most Senecan of all of Shakespeare's plays'.[2] Scholars and critics have pointed out affinities with Seneca in the structural and rhetorical features of the play, as well as in those less easily definable aspects which are usually grouped together as 'atmosphere': the presence in action or language, or both, of night, blood and the supernatural.[3] A number of verbal resemblances to lines in Seneca (both the original tragedies and the translations in the *Tenne Tragedies*) have also been pointed out, and especially *Agamemnon*, *Hercules Furens* and *Hippolytus* (or *Phaedra*) have thus been suggested as sources for *Macbeth*. Some critics feel that in preparation for writing *Macbeth* Shakespeare may have read, or re-read, at least part of Seneca's dramatic works;[4] and one of them thinks that, as most of the verbal echoes are from the *Hippolytus* and the *Hercules Furens*—both plays in which 'the protagonist's crimes are accompanied or followed by violent fear and remorse'—this indicates that Shakespeare, in turning to Seneca, paid particular attention to those plays which, compared with the others, he found 'closer in spirit to the theme he had chosen for his next drama'.[5] This may sound too deliberate an imitative process to those who like to think of the workings of Shakespeare's imagination as being less conscious. But the argument can, I think, be supported by the possibility—we are, of course, dealing with possibilities rather than facts—that another Senecan play, the *Medea*, contributed in a similar way towards the creation of *Macbeth*: a contribution traceable by some faint verbal echoes and a central thematic similarity.

It has been suggested at various times, and usually with hesitation, that lines from the *Medea* may be echoed in the witch-broth scene (IV, i) and in Lady Macbeth's appeal to the spirits of murder (I, v, 40–54).[6] I do not think that any verbal resemblances by themselves make up a significant claim for a connexion between the *Medea* and *Macbeth*.[7] On the other hand, the *Medea* seems to me to present a case where Shakespeare, whether from re-reading the play or from his memory of it, found some Senecan dramatic moments a help towards crystallizing and articulating a main motif in his play. From the way in which he uses Seneca at other points in the play, we can tell that—at least at this stage in his career—Shakespeare saw Seneca's plays not as storehouses of plot and character material, but as ways of analysing and defining emotional situations. We can also see that he draws on Seneca at important moments in the play. Thus, for example, it is well known that Macbeth's reaction to the stain of Duncan's blood on his hands—

> Will all great Neptune's ocean wash this blood
> Clean from my hand?— (II, ii, 59–60)

is an amalgamation of two passages from the *Hippolytus* (lines 715–18) and the *Hercules Furens* (lines 1323–9), respectively. The situations in which those two passages occur are very different between themselves: the first registers Hippolytus' revulsion as he throws from him the sword which he sees as polluted by Phaedra's incestuous desire, the second expresses Hercules' despair as he wakes from his mad fury to find that he has killed his wife and children; and neither, especially not the *Hippolytus* piece, is at all close in plot and character to the *Macbeth* situation. But Shakespeare's imagination must have been stirred by this image as a way of defining someone's realization that an act of sin is irreversible. His own elaboration on the basic image—

> No, this my hand will rather
> The multitudinous seas incarnadine,
> Making the green one red— (II, ii, 60–2)

shows just how vividly it has been stirred. What is more, the 'borrowed' image becomes part of a whole complex of themes in the play. It looks forward to Lady Macbeth's compulsive attempts to wash the 'damned spot', the 'smell of the blood' off *her* hand; and it recurs, as a whole river of blood, to measure Macbeth's departure further and further from Grace:

> I am in blood
> Stepp'd in so far, that, should I wade no more,
> Returning were as tedious as go o'er. (III, iv, 135–7)

These lines, while defining the emotional and moral state of Macbeth at that moment, are yet also, as F. R. Johnson points out,[8] a transmutation of that most famous Senecan tag from the *Agamemnon*, Clytemnestra's *sententia*,

> per scelera semper sceleribus tutum est iter.

I have laboured what may seem obvious, in order to outline my own argument: that, in the writing of *Macbeth*, the *Medea* may have been active in much the same way as we know other Senecan plays to have been; that Shakespeare has seized on a few emotional key-moments in the *Medea*, linked them with other themes and images in the play, and built them into his own moral structure. In drawing attention, then, to what I think may be a neglected source of *Macbeth*, I want not only to suggest another instance of Senecan imitation in the play but also to show another instance of how mature Shakespearian imitation of Seneca contains within itself a reaction away from Seneca.

Shakespeare's narrative source material—Holinshed and Buchanan—provided him both with the outline and with details of the action. It also provided him with the outline of Lady Macbeth, as an ambitious wife urging her initially only partly willing husband on to kill the king. The shaping vision which turned chronicle into poetic drama was one of evil—of, as G. Wilson Knight and many critics after him have shown, evil seen as perversions of the natural state in the individual, the family, the body politic and the universe. The two great thematic speeches which fit Lady Macbeth into this vision are, first, the invocation which follows on her reading of Macbeth's letter about the prophecies of the Weird Sisters—

> Come, you Spirits
> That tend on mortal thoughts, unsex me here;
> And fill me, from the crown to the toe, top-full
> Of direst cruelty! make thick my blood,

Stop up th' access and passage to remorse;
That no compunctious visitings of Nature
Shake my fell purpose, nor keep peace between
Th' effect and it. Come to my woman's breasts,
And take my milk for gall, you murth'ring ministers,
Wherever in your sightless substances
You wait on nature's mischief. Come, thick night,
And pall thee in the dunnest smoke of hell,
That my keen knife see not the wound it makes,
Nor Heaven peep through the blanket of the dark,
To cry 'Hold, hold'—   (I, v, 40–54)

and, secondly, the lines with which she whets Macbeth's blunting purpose:

I have given suck, and know
How tender 'tis to love the babe that milks me:
I would, while it was smiling in my face,
Have pluck'd my nipple from his boneless gums,
And dash'd the brains out, had I so sworn
As you have done to this.   (I, vii, 54–8)

In the first speech, Lady Macbeth rejects her very nature as a woman, turns her aim from creation of life to its destruction. The second treats the same theme on a more concrete, intimate and domestic level—and its evocation of natural disorder is all the more horrifying for it. Seneca has one woman whose action, in spirit if not in fact, is identical, and that is Medea.

In the opening scene of her play, Medea invokes Hecate, the goddess of night, hell and magic, to help her revenge herself on Jason by killing the king and the whole royal stock. Studley then makes her also envisage the slaying of her own children—

Then at the Aulters of the Gods my chyldren shalbe slayne,
With crimsen colourde bloud of Babes their Aulters will I stayne . . .

whereupon she goes on to ask, in an invocation to her own soul, to be unsexed:

If any lusty lyfe as yet within thy soule doe rest,
If ought of auncient corage still doe dwell within my brest,
Exile all foolysh Female feare, and pity from thy mynde,
And as th'untamed Tygers use to rage and rave unkynde . . .

                    . . . permit to lodge and rest,
Such salvage brutish tyranny within thy brasen brest.
What ever hurly burly wrought doth Phasis understand,
What mighty monstrous bloudy feate I wrought by Sea or Land,
The like in Corynth shalbe seene in most outragious guise,
Most hyddious, hatefull, horrible, to heare, or see wyth eyes,
Most divelish, desperate, dreadfull deede, yet never knowne before,
Whose rage shall force heaven, earth, and hell to quake and tremble sore . . .

As weyghty things as these I did in greener girlishe age,
Now sorrowes smart doth rub the gall and frets with sharper rage,
But sith my wombe hath yeelded fruict, it doth mee well behove,
The strength and parlous puissance of weightier illes to prove . . .

How wilt thou from thy spouse depart? as him thou followed hast
In bloud to bath thy bloudy handes and traytrous lyves to wast.

(*Tenne Tragedies*, II, 57)[9]

When we penetrate the blanket of Studley's rhetoric here, we find, in close proximity and linked in a similar train of associations, the main ideas and images of the Lady Macbeth passages. We also find ideas and images which, in *Macbeth*, link Lady Macbeth's speeches with the rest of the play. First of all, of course, Medea's lines share with Lady Macbeth's 'unsex me here' speech the framework of ritual incantation—which is handed on, as it were, to Macbeth himself in his invocation to Night before the murder of Banquo (III, iii, 46–50). (Nor may it be altogether irrelevant that, as Macbeth goes to murder Duncan, he envisages witchcraft celebrating 'pale Hecate's off'rings', II, 1, 51–2.) Within this rhetorical pattern, Medea's thoughts move from witchcraft, to royal murder, and to the slaying of her own children, with the courage and cruelty which this requires. The key-line comes in her desire to lose her woman's nature— stressing the 'feare, and pity' which we know are thematic words in *Macbeth*—and a little later this recurs in the cruel paradox that the very fact of her having been the source of life ('but sith my wombe hath yeelded fruict') is being turned into a further reason to kill. But before then we have heard how, unsexed and tigerish, she will do bloody deeds, too terrible (as is the case with both Macbeth and Lady Macbeth) to 'see wyth eyes', and how these deeds, 'shall force heaven, earth and hell to quake and tremble sore', in the kind of universal confusion which Macbeth envisages in the witch-scene, IV, i (lines 50–61). The Medea passage leads up to the central *Macbeth* image of hands bathed in blood—common enough, by itself, in Senecan and Elizabethan tragedy, but significant as the end-product of this particular piece of unnatural 'argument'. There is no reference to milk or giving suck here, to correspond with the second of Lady Macbeth's speeches; but in Act IV of the *Medea*—where indeed 'witchcraft celebrates pale Hecate's off'rings'—there is a scene which is bound to have struck a reader as an emblem of unnatural womanhood and in which a mother's breast is linked with the massacre of her own tender children. Medea, with her breasts bared, sheds her own blood as a sacrifice to Hecate, so that she may harden herself to that massacre:

With naked breast and dugges layde out Ile pricke with sacred blade
Myne arme, that for the bubling bloude an issue may bee made,
With trilling streames my purple bloude let drop on Th'aulter stones.
My tender Childrens crusshed fleshe, and broken brooosed bones
Lerne how to brooke with hardned heart: in practise put the trade
To florishe fearce, and keepe a coyle, with naked glittring blade.

(*Tenne Tragedies*, II, 90)[10]

In terms of plot and character *Medea* is a play of sexual jealousy and of terrible revenge taken by a wife on a husband and has as little in common with *Macbeth* as the crude horror of Studley's rhetoric has in common with the poetry of the 'I have given suck' speech. But in terms of tragic emotion the play centres on an obsessed woman perverting her woman's nature in order to do the most unnatural of all deeds, kill her own children—though pity, in the shape of her babes, stands literally before her. It may be objected here that to the Elizabethan imagination Medea was a witch, and that that image would overlay any others in the play. Certainly the Medea of Ovid's *Metamorphoses* (Book VII) was a witch. Ovid, naturally stressing those events in the myth which involve transformations, dwells at length on how Medea aids Jason in getting the golden fleece, how she rejuvenates old Aeson (as Shakespeare remembered in *The Merchant of Venice*, V, i, 13–15) and makes the daughters of Pelias kill their aged father, while he hurries over the events in Corinth in the briefest possible way. Ben Jonson in *The Masque of Queens* used the incantations of Seneca's Medea and of Ovid's side by side.[11] In Cooper's *Thesaurus* the entry on Medea has not a word about her killing of her own children. But the Elizabethan imagination also admitted another Medea image, and that was one of the unnatural woman and damned sinner. Thus in Richard Robinson's singularly pedestrian Mirror-work, *The Rewarde of Wickednesse* (published in 1574), Medea, who is suffering torments in hell, narrates her story from the point of view of 'how I did nature quite forsake'.[12] She acted, she says,

> by Deuillishe ways as women shoulde not doe
> For why they ought with mercye to bee milde,
> and not theyr wicked willes for to pursue.   (fol. 3 v)

And in the conclusion of the poem—'the bookes verdite vpon Medea'—we hear, in lines which, for all their crudeness, might remind one of Lady Macbeth's readiness to dash out the brains of her smiling babe, how she

> her Children deare, hath wounde with mortall knife,
> The smiling Babes her body beare, bereft their tender life.

Obviously I am not suggesting that Shakespeare was echoing the poetry, if it can be so called, of Richardson; but these lines show the kind of image the Senecan Medea figure would leave on the imagination. Studley—who in the dedicatory epistle to the 1566 edition of his *Medea* translation presents Seneca as 'yᵗ pearlesse Poet and most Christian Ethnicke'—reinforces the impression which Seneca's original gives: that, though the witch-practices of Medea take up most of Act IV and are referred to throughout, they are peripheral to the real tragic action in which Medea is a wilfully wicked moral agent. Studley constantly 'places' her by the word 'wicked'; without any foundation at all in the original he will sometimes make her speak of her 'wicked will'; and in the struggle between her womanly pity and her desire to kill her children in revenge, he translates Seneca's lines,

> ira pietatem fugat
> iramque pietas,   (lines 943–4)

into a morality struggle between vice and virtue:

> Wrath sometyme chaseth vertue out, and vertue wrath agayne.
>   (*Tenne Tragedies*, p. 95)

57

Above all, Studley's version of the last line in the play makes it a fitting end to a tragedy of damnation:

Beare witnesse, grace of God is none in place of thy repayre.

(Tenne Tragedies, p. 98)

As a rendering of Seneca's words, 'testare nullos esse, qua veheris, deos', this has been praised by T. S. Eliot,[13] but it is clearly a twist of the original meaning: a moralistic reading of the nihilist curse of Jason.

The woman damning herself by unnatural acts was, of course, not new in *Macbeth*. In the two speeches quoted, Lady Macbeth performs in ritual a rejection of womanhood which Goneril and Regan had acted out in their deeds, and which speeches about them had drawn attention to:

Tigers, not daughters, what have you perform'd?

Thou changed and self-cover'd thing, for shame,
Be-monster not thy feature . . .

. . . howe'er thou art a fiend,
A woman's shape doth shield thee.　　　　*(King Lear, IV, ii, 40–68)*

When Lear curses Goneril for her unkindness, he strikes at the very essence of her womanhood, unsexing her as Lady Macbeth is to unsex herself:

Hear Nature, hear; dear goddess, hear.
Suspend thy purpose, if thou didst intend
To make this creature fruitful.
Into her womb convey sterility;
Dry up in her the organs of increase;
And from her derogate body never spring
A babe to honour her!　　　　*(I, iv, 275–81)*

Yet the unwomanliness of Goneril and Regan differs from Lady Macbeth's not only because they literally reject their father whereas Lady Macbeth symbolically rejects her children; it differs, too, because it is existential—consequent upon their actions of unkindness. In Lady Macbeth it is essential: it is—as in Medea—the deliberate and rhetorically articulated point from which, on her first appearance in the play, all her acts (and, in a sense, those of Macbeth, for in unsexing herself she mothers his deeds) proceed.

Some of the links in the chain of associated images and ideas which connect *Macbeth* with the *Medea* are not very unique or far-fetched. Shakespeare had dealt with rejection of pity, murderous cruelty (exercised on innocent children) and unwomanliness much earlier. Interestingly, however, one of the earliest occurrences in Shakespeare of a combination of these ideas suggests that he already associated the Medea story with a particular kind of destructiveness. In *2 Henry VI* there is the following reference to the story of how Medea slew and dismembered her brother Absyrtus:

Meet I an infant of the house of York,
Into as many gobbets will I cut it
As wild Medea young Absyrtus did:
In cruelty will I seek out my fame.　　　　*(V, ii, 57–60)*

It has generally been assumed that the source of this passage is in Ovid's *Tristia*, III, ix.[14] An English source has been suggested by Starnes and Talbert, who quote Cooper's summary of the story in his *Thesaurus*:

... she ranne away with Jason and tooke with her Absyrtus hir yong brother ... Medea seeing that nothing coud stay hir fathers haste, fearing to be taken, kylled the yong babe hir brother, and scattered his lymmes in the way as hir father should passe. With sorrow whereof and long seeking the partes of his yong sonnes bodye the father was stayed and Jason with Medea in the meane tyme escaped out of his realme.[15]

Starnes and Talbert point out that Cooper's version shares with the passage in *2 Henry VI* an emphasis on the *infancy* of Absyrtus which is lacking in Ovid. They also suggest that the 'gobbets' of the Shakespearian passage derive from Cooper's expression 'partes of his yong sonnes body'. But a more direct and plausible source seems to me to be the account of this episode in Seneca's *Medea*, which in the Studley translation reads like this:

> My tender Brother eke, that with my Syer did mee pursue,
> Whom with his secret partes cut of, I wicked Virgin slewe,
> Whose shreaded and dismembred corps, with sword in gobbits hewd,
> (A wofull Coarse to th' Fathers heart) on Pontus ground I strewd.
>
> (*Tenne Tragedies*, p. 61)

Neither Studley nor the original Latin ever mention the boy by name (Seneca, quite clear about his infancy, refers to him as 'nefandae virginis parvus comes'), so the *Medea* cannot be Shakespeare's only source of knowledge for the allusion. But the youth of the boy is stressed just as much as in the Cooper passage, and above all the verbal parallelism in the cutting of the boy's body into 'gobbets'—a favourite Studley word for describing pieces of dismembered human anatomy—suggests that these lines may lie behind Shakespeare's.[16] Anyone who read the *Medea* would be repeatedly reminded of the murder of Absyrtus; Medea refers to it no less than eleven times, and in the end it is her vision of Absyrtus' ghosts which ends her hesitation and drives her to the murder of her own children:

> Alas they [her children] bee mere innocents, I doe not this denay:
> So was my brother whom I slew ...
>
> Yet for my sire and brother, twayne I have, there needes no more ...
>
> My slaughtred brothers ghost it is that vengaunce coms to crave.
>
> (*Tenne Tragedies*, pp. 95–6)

The Absyrtus passage in *2 Henry VI* is the one where Young Clifford discovers his dead father. It is part of a speech which opens with what A. S. Cairncross calls 'a regular Shakespearian group of images': the discovery of a death leads to the idea that chaos has come again.[17] The lines have the ring of mature Shakespeare:

> O! let the vile world end,
> And the premised flames of the last day
> Knit earth and heaven together;

> Now let the general trumpet blow his blast,
> Particularities and petty sounds
> To cease!
>
> (v, ii, 40–5)

They anticipate Macduff's reaction to the murder of Duncan (*Macbeth*, II, iii, 63–81). It is therefore all the more interesting that the next set of images in the speech—deliberate rejection of pity and the murder of innocent children—

> Even at this sight
> My heart is turn'd to stone: and while 'tis mine
> It shall be stony. York not our old men spares;
> No more will I their babes . . .
>
> Henceforth I will not have to do with pity:
> Meet I an infant of the house of York . . .
>
> (v, ii, 49–57)

is linked with Medea (and, as I have tried to show, probably with Seneca's *Medea*). Though the overt association disappears after this passage, I have a strong feeling that it continues, as it were, underground to enrich the texture of the episodes of *2* and *3 Henry VI* which are consequent on this scene. In the actual killing of young Rutland, which is what the Absyrtus speech anticipates, the 'innocent child' pleads with Clifford for his life, and Clifford replies in words which, on the one hand, suggest Medea's argument of a brother and a father for two sons, and, on the other, look forward to *Macbeth*. Clifford's words,

> In vain thou speak'st, poor boy; my father's blood
> Hath stopp'd the passage where thy words should enter,
>
> (*3 Henry VI*, I, iii, 21–2)

should be compared with Lady Macbeth's,

> Make thick my blood,
> Stop up th' access and passage to remorse.

Young Clifford's ally, Queen Margaret, is often—like Tamora in *Titus Andronicus*—referred to somewhat loosely as a 'Senecan woman'. In the particular chain of associations which I am tracing, that 'tiger's heart wrapt in a woman's hide' adds the notion of murderous cruelty and (virtually) child-murder as manifestation of unnatural womanhood. The baiting of York (*3 Henry VI*, I, iv) is akin to the scene where Medea confronts Jason with his dead sons; and it turns in its climax on the un-womanliness of Margaret:

> How could'st thou drain the life-blood of the child,
> To bid the father wipe his eyes withal,
> And yet be seen to bear a woman's face?
> Women are soft, mild, pitiful, and flexible;
> Thou stern, indurate, flinty, rough, remorseless . . .
>
> But you are more inhuman, more inexorable—
> O, ten times more—than tigers of Hyrcania.
>
> (I, iv, 138–55)

60

There was clearly no need, either here or in the similar passage in *Titus Andronicus*, II, iii, 136–60 (in which the breast-feeding image also appears, to define Tamora's unnaturalness), to go to the *Medea* for the image of a woman turned tiger; yet, in the context of other Medean associations, it may be worth remembering that in the first of the *Medea* speeches quoted above she sees herself, when unsexed, as one of 'th'untamed Tygers' which 'rage and rave unkynde'.

Various resemblances between *Macbeth* and *2* and *3 Henry VI* have previously been noted,[18] and to these, I think, might be added a common kinship with Seneca's *Medea*. Needless to say, the nature and degree of that kinship are very different: in the *Henry VI* scenes (as in the *Titus Andronicus* one, referred to above) there is that dramatic interest in evil sadistically enjoyed which characterizes the end of the *Medea*—

> This onely is the thing that wants unto my wicked will,
> That Jasons eyes should see this sight as yet I doe suppose,
> Nothing it is that I have done, my travell all I lose,
> That I employde in dyry deedes, unlesse he see the same—
>
> (*Tenne Tragedies*, p. 97)

and which is epitomized in Atreus' words about Thyestes:

> miserum videre nolo, sed dum fit miser.   (*Thyestes*, line 907)

Macbeth has none of this quality: evil is presented here, on the one·hand, in terms of its workings in the minds of Macbeth and Lady Macbeth and, on the other, as part of a larger moral and metaphysical pattern. Seneca begins and ends with the mind and deeds of Medea, and although a general destructiveness is one aspect of these—

> Then onely can I be at rest, when every thing I see
> Throwne headlong topsie turvey downe to ruthfull ende with me.
> With mee let all things cleane decay: thy selfe if thou doe spill,
> Thou maist drive to destruction what else with thee thou will—
>
> (*Tenne Tragedies*, p. 74)

he does not, like Shakespeare, through structure and imagery build up a pattern in which the protagonist is seen as one manifestation of universal evil. To take just one example, there is in Seneca none of that inclusiveness of vision whereby in *Macbeth*, after Macbeth's Medea-like words,

> . . . though the treasure
> Of nature's germens tumble all together,
> Even till destruction sicken—answer me
> To what I ask you,   (IV, i, 58–61)

the first thing that goes into the witches' brew is 'sow's blood, that hath eaten / Her nine farrow' —a gruesome beast version of Lady Macbeth's symbolical slaying of her own child, linking the wife's destructiveness with the husband's into a coherent whole. On this point, the *Henry VI* plays are much closer to *Macbeth* than they are to *Medea*. Although in these early histories each scene tends to be a climax in itself, Shakespeare is beginning to articulate the chronicle material into a moral pattern. The world in which women turn into tigers and prey on innocent children is the world defined in the emblematic scene in *3 Henry VI* (II, v) where enter a son that has

61

killed his father and a father that has killed his son. From the scene where the queen's side confront the sons of York—*3 Henry VI*, II, ii, a scene thick with references to the atrocities committed by either side, but most of all to the 'butcher'-like killing of 'our tender brother Rutland'—there emerges, in the prince's words, a world in the same moral confusion as that evoked by the witches' 'fair is foul, and foul is fair':

> If that be right which Warwick says is right,
> There is no wrong, but every thing is right.   (II, ii, 131–2)

The image of the son who has killed his father and the father who has killed his son is a self-conscious pointing of the pattern; in *Macbeth* the pattern, as so many critics have shown, grows naturally out of a fusion of action and imagery. Macbeth kills his king (and father-figure) Duncan and accuses Duncan's sons of having killed their father and so creates a world where day is turned into night and horses eat each other. And at the centre of this disorder stands Lady Macbeth who in two speeches has unsexed herself and symbolically slain her issue.

In an interesting article on 'The Sources of *Macbeth*' (in this volume), Professor M. C. Bradbrook suggested that Shakespeare got the inspiration for those two speeches from chapter xiii of the *Description of Scotland* prefixed to Holinshed's *Chronicle*:

. . . each woman would take intolerable pains to bring up and nourish her own children. They thought them furthermore not to be kindly fostered, except they were so well nourished after their births with the milk of their breasts as they were before they were born with the blood of their own bellies: nay, they feared lest they should degenerate and grow out of kind, except they gave them suck themselves, and eschewed strange milk, therefore in labour and painfulness they were equal [i.e. with the fighting men] . . . In these days also the women of our country were of no less courage than the men, for all stout maids and wives (if they were not with child) marched as well into the field as did the men, and so soon as the army did set forward, they slew the first living creature that they found, in whose blood they not only bathed their swords, but also tasted thereof with their mouths, with no less religion and assurance conceived, than if they had already been sure of some notable and fortunate victory.[19]

Dr Bradbrook finds in this passage the 'intimate relation between tenderness and barbarity' which she thinks gives us the 'fundamental character of Lady Macbeth as it is embodied in the most frightful of her speeches'. It seems to me very likely that Shakespeare knew the *Description of Scotland*, and that he may have been impressed by the above passage; but I do not think it gives us the fundamental point of those two speeches. The point of the relation between tenderness and war-like courage in the *Description* is that they co-existed, that they were both aspects of womanhood—albeit a primitive or barbaric version of it. The barbarity of those early Scotswomen did not exercise itself at the expense of procreation—it is especially stressed that women with child did not join in the fighting—or of child-nursing. The unnatural paradox of Lady Macbeth's speeches is the fact that she is ready to give up her womanhood to murder, her milk to gall, to kill her smiling babe in order to live up to a destructive oath. These are the qualities epitomized by Medea, and foreshadowed by Albany when he sees, as the outcome of Goneril's rejection of her womanhood, how

> Humanity must perforce prey on itself,
> Like monsters of the deep.   (*King Lear*, IV, ii, 47–9)

The last thing envisaged in the *Description* is Scottish humanity preying on *itself*. Nor does *Macbeth* as a whole bear out the Amazonian concept of womanhood which the *Description* suggests. The only other woman whom we see, Lady Macduff, is tender and mild and 'womanly' —the 'dam' for the 'pretty chickens' of Macduff. When Ross tells Malcolm that, if he would return to Scotland, this

> Would create soldiers, make our women fight,
> To doff their dire distresses, (IV, iii, 187–8)

this is the measure of the extremity of a situation which demands extreme means, not a reference to a natural state of affairs. Indeed, Lady Macbeth's essential perversion of womanhood is ironically stressed by the way other characters in the play expect her to conform to its natural mode. Not only does Duncan several times refer to her in terms such as 'most kind hostess', but when the murder of the king has been discovered, Macduff tries to spare her:

> O gentle lady,
> 'Tis not for you to hear what I can speak!
> The repetition in a woman's ear
> Would murder as it fell. (II, iii, 83–6)

But the deepest irony of all is that her woman's nature does in the end steal up on her: she who had sacrificed her womanhood for the deed finds herself destroyed by the memory of the deed. And within the same pattern, Macbeth, who through her has deprived himself of issue, finds himself defeated by the issue of Banquo.

We are here at the point where the ways of Shakespeare and of Seneca utterly part. In Shakespeare's structure, Lady Macbeth's Medea-like action is doubly defeated: first by the self-destructiveness of evil—humanity turning away from woman- and man-hood, into beasts, and thus preying, by the natural order, on itself—and secondly by the positive power of good, as symbolized by the bloody babe (bloody, not because its brains have been dashed out but because of a victorious birth) and by Banquo's issue stretching out to the crack of doom; and as seen in action by the return of Malcolm. While Medea finds her heroic self *through* evil, the two Macbeths lose themselves through evil. Shakespeare's woman unwomanized becomes 'fiend-like' and hence less than a woman; Seneca's becomes a heroine and hence more than a woman. The *Medea* is a study of destruction, an analysis of evil, and there is no suggestion in Jason's concluding curse that 'the time is free'. Shakespeare's vision of evil included a vision of the defeat of that evil, of what G. Wilson Knight has called 'a wrestling of destruction with creation'.[20] We cannot say whether Shakespeare's fiendlike queen would have been possible without Seneca, but we can say that an imaginative understanding of the total meaning of such fiend-likeness—of all the implications of 'unsex me here'—would not have been possible without Shakespeare.

NOTES

1. C. Mendell, *Our Seneca* (Yale University Press, 1941), p. 199.

2. *The Royal Play of 'Macbeth'* (New York, 1950), p. 48.

3. See, for example, J. W. Cunliffe, *The Influence of Seneca on Elizabethan Tragedy* (1893); F. L. Lucas, *Seneca and Elizabethan Tragedy* (Cambridge, 1922); T. S. Eliot's Introduction to *Seneca, his Tenne Tragedies* . . . (The Tudor Translations, 2nd ser., 1927), reprinted in *Selected Essays*; Hardin Craig, 'The Shackling of Accidents', *P.Q.* XIX (1940), 1–19; J. M. Nosworthy, 'The Bleeding Captain Scene in *Macbeth*', *R.E.S.* XXII (1946), 126–30.

4. See Kenneth Muir, *Shakespeare's Sources* (1957), p. 180; and N. Fleming, 'The Influence of Seneca on Shakespeare', unpublished M.A. Dissertation, in the Liverpool University Library (1956).

5. Francis R. Johnson, 'Shakespearian Imagery and Senecan Imitation', *John Quincy Adams Memorial Studies*, ed. J. McManaway (Washington, 1948), p. 44.

6. See Cunliffe, *op. cit.* p. 46; Mendell, *op. cit.* p. 199; Fleming, *op. cit.* p. 201.

7. There are some similarities between the ingredients of Medea's potion (Act IV) and those of the *Hexenkessel* in *Macbeth*; but, as far as classical influence behind this scene goes, it is equally possible (as, for example, Paul thinks: *op. cit.* p. 262) that Shakespeare had in mind the brew prepared by Ovid's Medea (*Metamorphoses*, VII, 215–93). It seems to me impossible to be sure about verbal dependencies here—especially as Seneca presumably himself drew on Ovid. In Elizabethan literature the lines of Ovid's Medea are often conflated with those of Seneca's, and also with those of that other Senecan witch, the Nurse in *Hercules Oetaeus*. An example of this may be found in Prospero's speech in *The Tempest*, V, i, 33–50, which scholars agree shows Shakespeare using Ovid both in the original Latin and in Golding's translation. T. W. Baldwin (*William Shakspere's Small Latine and Lesse Greeke*, 1944, II, 447) thinks that the line 'I have bedimm'd / The noontide sun' shows Shakespeare echoing Golding's version of Ovid's 'currus quoque carmine nostro / pallet': 'Our Sorcerie dimmes the Morning faire, and darkes the Sun at Noone'. In Ovid, Baldwin points out, the sun appears only by allusion, and there is nothing specifically to suggest noon. But, verbally, Shakespeare's line could equally be paralleled—it seems to me—by Studley's version of line 768 in Seneca's *Medea*—'Phoebus in medio stetit': 'I rolling up the magicke verse at noone time Phoebus stay'—which has

both sun and 'noon'; and by Studley's line in *Hercules Oetaeus* (*Tenne Tragedies*, II, 211), in which Deianira describes the effect of the 'magicke vearse' of the Nurse: 'And noonetyde topsy turvy tost doth dim the dusky day', and which has both 'dim' and 'noontide'.

8. F. R. Johnson, *op. cit.* pp. 50–2.

9. I quote from the Tudor Translations edition of *Seneca, his Tenne Tragedies*, II, 53–98. The passage quoted is Studley's rendering of the following lines in Seneca (quoted from the Loeb ed.):

> si vivis, anime, si quid antiqui tibi
> remanet vigoris; pelle femineos metus
> et inhospitalem Caucasum mente indue.
> quodcumque vidit Pontus aut Phasis nefas,
> videbit Isthmos. effera ignota horrida,
> tremenda caelo pariter ac terris mala
> mens intus agitat—vulnera et caedem et vagum
> funus per artus. levia memoravi nimis;
> haec virgo feci. gravior exurgat dolor;
> maiora iam me scelera post partus decent.
> accingere ira teque in exitium para
> furore toto. paria narrentur tua
> repudia thalamis. quo virum linques modo?
> hoc quo secuta es.   (41–54)

Apart from the fact that Studley considerably elaborates upon the manifestations of Medea's wrath (in the lines I have left out), he also adds lines or phrases which suggest that it is the translation, rather than the original, which may lie behind *Macbeth*. Seneca has nothing corresponding to the two first quoted Studley lines, about the slaying of Medea's own children. He does not emphasize the unsexing, as Studley does: above all, it is only fear—'femineos metus'—not 'pity', that his Medea wants to be free from. The brief Senecan reference to Medea's motherhood—'post partus'—is developed by Studley into a concrete 'sith my wombe hath yeelded fruict' (more akin to Lady Macbeth's 'I have given suck'). Studley, unlike Seneca, makes Medea envisage deeds too horrible to 'see with eyes'. And, finally, there is no immediate Senecan source in this passage for Studley's climactic and *Macbeth*-like image of hands bathed in blood.

10. Studley's rendering of lines 805–10 in Seneca's *Medea*:

> tibi nudato
> pectore maenas sacro feriam
> bracchia cultro. manet noster
> sanguis ad aras; assuesce, manus,
> stringere ferrum carosque pati
> posse cruores.

As in the previous passage, Studley here heavily elaborates, over Seneca, the situation of a woman and mother performing an unnatural deed. Seneca has the grim paradox of the heroine hardening herself to shed 'caros ... cruores'; but Studley not only introduces the vivid image of the 'tender Childrens crusshed fleshe' but also contrasts this with the emphatic description of the bared breast ('and dugges layde out'). Grim as the artistic effect is, the emotional impact is more powerfully human than is Seneca's magic ritual.

11. See his marginal gloss to *The Masque of Queens* (*Ben Jonson*, ed. Herford and Simpson, Oxford, 1941, VII, 294–5 and 299).

12. *The rewarde of Wickednesse Discoursing the sundrye monstrous abuses of wicked and vngodlye worldelinges ... With a liuely description of their seuerall falles and finall destruction ...* by Richard Robinson (1574). As Shakespeare echoes *The Rape of Lucrece* in *Macbeth* (cf. new Arden *Macbeth*, ed. Kenneth Muir, Appendix D), it may be worth noting that, in Robinson's picture of hell, the sinner exhibited immediately before Medea is 'young *Tarquin* rewarded for his wickednesse' of 'Pride and Whoredome' (fols. D3ᵛ–F2).

13. *Tenne Tragedies*, I, xvi, and *Selected Essays*, p. 59. A further indication of the moralizing note in Studley's version of the *Medea* is that he substitutes for the first Chorus, which is an epithalamium, a kind of Mirrorpoem on the wrongdoings of Jason and Medea.

14. See T. W. Baldwin, *Shakspere's Small Latine*, II, 429–30, and the notes on this passage in the New Shakespeare edition (ed. J. Dover Wilson, Cambridge, 1952) and the new Arden edition (ed. Andrew S. Cairncross, 1957) of *2 Henry VI*.

15. De Witt T. Starnes and Ernest W. Talbert, *Classical Myth and Legend in Renaissance Dictionaries* (Chapel Hill, 1955), p. 112.

16. For 'gobbets'—which word occurs in the same play at IV, 1, 85—H. C. Hart (Arden edition of *2 Henry VI*, 1909) refers to two occurrences in Golding and one in *The Faerie Queene*; but its use here in the Absyrtus context would seem to indicate Studley as a source.

17. New Arden edition, p. 151. The version of this speech in *The Contention*, which Cairncross believes to be a memorial reconstruction, is much more 'Senecan' in the sense of heavily rhetorical; but it has not got the Absyrtus image. Dover Wilson, who is sceptical about Shakespeare's hand in much of *2 Henry VI*, believes that Shakespeare has 'revised pretty thoroughly' (New Shakespeare edition, p. 195) this part of the play.

18. See new Arden *Macbeth*, ed. Kenneth Muir, Appendix D.

19. P. 17 above.

20. *The Imperial Theme* (1931), p. 153. Cf. also Cleanth Brooks, 'The Naked Babe and the Cloak of Manliness', *The Well Wrought Urn* (1949).

IMAGE AND SYMBOL IN *MACBETH*

BY

KENNETH MUIR

A good deal has been written about the imagery of *Macbeth* since Caroline Spurgeon showed[1] that the iterative image was that of a man in ill-fitting garments. It has been pointed out, for example, that the image can be interpreted in more than one way and that we need not necessarily suppose that Shakespeare looked on his hero as a small man in garments too large for him: we may rather suppose that the point of the image is that the garments were stolen or that they symbolize the hypocrisy to which Macbeth is reluctantly committed when he embarks on his career of crime. It has also been pointed out[2] that this particular image should be considered in relation to a wider group of tailoring images, of which the imaginary tailor, admitted by the Porter of Hell-gate, may be regarded as a kind of patron.[3]

What is more important is that, since the publication of R. B. Heilman's books on *King Lear* and *Othello*,[4] W. H. Clemen's *The Development of Shakespeare's Imagery* and G. Wilson Knight's series of interpretations, Miss Spurgeon's concentration on a single iterative image, even though numerically predominant, is apt to be misleading. The total meaning of each play depends on a complex of interwoven patterns and the imagery must be considered in relation to character and structure.

One group of images to which Cleanth Brooks called attention was that concerned with babes.[5] It has been suggested[6] by Muriel C. Bradbrook that Shakespeare may have noticed in the general description of the manners of Scotland included in Holinshed's *Chronicles* that every Scotswoman 'would take intolerable pains to bring up and nourish her own children'; and H. N. Paul pointed out[7] that one of the topics selected for debate before James I, during his visit to Oxford in the summer of 1605, was whether a man's character was influenced by his nurse's milk. Whatever the origin of the images in *Macbeth* relating to breast-feeding, Shakespeare uses them for a very dramatic purpose. Their first appearance is in Lady Macbeth's invocation of the evil spirits to take possession of her:

> Come to my woman's breasts,
> And take my milk for gall, you murd'ring ministers,
> Wherever in your sightless substances
> You wait on nature's mischief.

They next appear in the scene where she incites Macbeth to the murder of Duncan:

> I have given suck, and know
> How tender 'tis to love the babe that milks me—
> I would, while it was smiling in my face,
> Have pluck'd my nipple from his boneless gums,
> And dash'd the brains out, had I so sworn as you
> Have done to this.

In between these two passages, Macbeth himself, debating whether to do the deed, admits that

> Pity, like a naked new-born babe
> Striding the blast,

would plead against it; and Lady Macbeth, when she first considers whether she can persuade her husband to kill Duncan, admits that she fears his nature:

> It is too full o' th' milk of human kindness
> To catch the nearest way.

Later in the play, Malcolm, when he is pretending to be worse even than Macbeth, says that he loves crime:

> Nay, had I pow'r, I should
> Pour the sweet milk of concord into hell,
> Uproar the universal peace, confound
> All unity on earth.

In these passages the babe symbolizes pity, and the necessity for pity, and milk symbolizes humanity, tenderness, sympathy, natural human feelings, the sense of kinship, all of which have been outraged by the murderers. Lady Macbeth can nerve herself to the deed only by denying her real nature; and she can overcome Macbeth's scruples only by making him ignore his feelings of human-kindness—his kinship with his fellow-men.

Cleanth Brooks suggests therefore that it is appropriate that one of the three apparitions should be a bloody child, since Macduff is converted into an avenger by the murder of his wife and babes. On one level, the bloody child stands for Macduff; on another level, it is the naked new-born babe whose pleadings Macbeth has ignored. Helen Gardner took Cleanth Brooks to task for considering these images in relation to one another.[8] She argued that in his comments on 'Pity, like a naked new-born babe' he had sacrificed

a Shakespearian depth of human feeling . . . by attempting to interpret an image by the aid of what associations it happens to arouse in him, and by being more interested in making symbols of babes fit each other than in listening to what Macbeth is saying. *Macbeth* is a tragedy and not a melodrama or a symbolic drama of retribution. The reappearance of 'the babe symbol' in the apparition scene and in Macduff's revelation of his birth has distracted the critic's attention from what deeply moves the imagination and the conscience in this vision of a whole world weeping at the inhumanity of helplessness betrayed and innocence and beauty destroyed. It is the judgment of the human heart that Macbeth fears here, and the punishment which the speech foreshadows is not that he will be cut down by Macduff, but that having murdered his own humanity he will enter a world of appalling loneliness, of meaningless activity, unloved himself, and unable to love.

Although this is both eloquent and true, it does not quite dispose of Brooks's interpretation of the imagery. Miss Gardner shows that, elsewhere in Shakespeare, 'a cherub is thought of as not only young, beautiful, and innocent, but as associated with the virtue of patience'; and that in the *Macbeth* passage the helpless babe and the innocent and beautiful cherub 'call out the pity and love by which Macbeth is judged. It is not terror of heaven's vengeance which makes him pause, but the terror of moral isolation.' Yet, earlier in the same speech Macbeth expresses fear of retribution in this life—fear that he himself will have to drink the ingredients of his own poisoned chalice—and his comparison of Duncan's virtues to 'angels, trumpet-tongued' implies a fear of judgment in the life to come, notwithstanding his boast that he would 'jump' it. We may assume, perhaps, that the discrepancy between the argument of the speech and the imagery employed is deliberate. On the surface Macbeth appears to be giving merely prudential reasons for not murdering Duncan; but Shakespeare makes him reveal by the imagery he employs that he, or his unconscious mind, is horrified by the thought of the deed to which he is being driven.[9]

Miss Gardner does not refer to the breast-feeding images—even Cleanth Brooks does not mention one of the most significant—yet all these images are impressive in their contexts and, taken together, they coalesce into a symbol of humanity, kinship and tenderness violated by Macbeth's crimes. Miss Gardner is right in demanding that the precise meaning and context of each image should be considered, but wrong, I believe, in refusing to see any significance in the group as a whole. *Macbeth*, of course, is a tragedy; but I know of no valid definition of tragedy which would prevent the play from being at the same time a symbolic drama of retribution.[10]

Another important group of images is concerned with sickness and medicine, and it is significant that they all appear in the last three acts of the play after Macbeth has ascended the throne; for Scotland is suffering from the disease of tyranny, which can be cured, as fever was thought to be cured, only by bleeding or purgation. The tyrant, indeed, uses sickness imagery of himself. He tells the First Murderer that so long as Banquo is alive he wears his health but sickly; when he hears of Fleance's escape he exclaims 'Then comes my fit again'; and he envies Duncan in the grave, sleeping after life's fitful fever, since life itself is one long illness. In the last act of the play a doctor, called in to diagnose Lady Macbeth's illness, confesses that he cannot

> minister to a mind diseas'd,
> Pluck from the memory a rooted sorrow,
> Raze out the written troubles of the brain,
> And with some sweet oblivious antidote
> Cleanse the stuff'd bosom of that perilous stuff
> Which weighs upon the heart.

Macbeth then professes to believe that what is amiss with Scotland is not his own evil tyranny but the English army of liberation:

> What rhubarb, cyme, or what purgative drug
> Would scour these English hence?

On the other side, the victims of tyranny look forward to wholesome days when Scotland will be freed. Malcolm says that Macbeth's very name blisters their tongues and he laments that 'each new day a gash' is added to Scotland's wounds. In the last act Caithness refers to Malcolm as 'the medicine of the sickly weal',

> And with him pour we in our country's purge
> Each drop of us.

Lennox adds:

> Or so much as it needs
> To dew the sovereign flower and drown the weeds.

68

Macbeth is the disease from which Scotland is suffering; Malcolm, the rightful king, is the *sovereign* flower, both royal and curative. Macbeth, it is said,

> Cannot buckle his distemper'd cause
> Within the belt of rule.

James I, in *A Counter-blast to Tobacco*, referred to himself as 'the proper Phisician of his Politicke-bodie', whose duty it was 'to purge it of all those diseases, by Medicines meet for the same'. It is possible that Shakespeare had read this pamphlet,[11] although, of course, disease-imagery is to be found in most of the plays written about this time. In *Hamlet* and *Coriolanus* it is applied to the body politic, as indeed it was by many writers on political theory. Shakespeare may have introduced the King's Evil as an allusion to James I's reluctant use of his supposed healing powers; but even without this topical reference, the incident provides a contrast to the evil supernatural represented by the Weird Sisters and is therefore dramatically relevant.

The contrast between good and evil is brought out in a variety of ways. There is not merely the contrast between the good and bad kings, which becomes explicit in the scene where Malcolm falsely accuses himself of avarice, lechery, cruelty and all of Macbeth's vices, and disclaims the possession of the king-becoming graces:

> Justice, verity, temperance, stableness,
> Bounty, perseverance, mercy, lowliness,
> Devotion, patience, courage, fortitude.

There is also a contrast throughout the play between the powers of light and darkness. It has often been observed that many scenes are set in darkness. Duncan arrives at Inverness as night falls; he is murdered during the night; Banquo returns from his last ride as night is again falling; Lady Macbeth has light by her continually; and even the daylight scenes during the first part of the play are mostly gloomy in their setting—a blasted heath, wrapped in mist, a dark cavern. The murder of Duncan is followed by darkness at noon—'dark night strangles the travelling lamp'. Before the murder Macbeth prays to the stars to hide their fires and Lady Macbeth invokes the night to conceal their crime:

> Come, thick night,
> And pall thee in the dunnest smoke of hell,
> That my keen knife see not the wound it makes,
> Nor heaven peep through the blanket of the dark
> To cry 'Hold, hold'.

Macbeth, as he goes towards the chamber of the sleeping Duncan, describes how

> o'er the one half-world
> Nature seems dead, and wicked dreams abuse
> The curtain'd sleep.

The word 'night' echoes through the first two scenes of the third act; and Macbeth invokes night to conceal the murder of Banquo:

> Come, seeling night,
> Scarf up the tender eye of pitiful day . . .
> Light thickens, and the crow
> Makes wing to th' rooky wood;
> Good things of day begin to droop and drowse,
> Whiles night's black agents to their preys do rouse.

In the scene in England and in the last act of the play—except for the sleep-walking scene—the darkness is replaced by light.

The symbolism is obvious. In many of these contexts night and darkness are associated with evil, and day and light are linked with good. The 'good things of day' are contrasted with 'night's black agents'; and, in the last act, day stands for the victory of the forces of liberation (v, iv, 1; v, vii, 27; v, viii, 37). The 'midnight hags' are 'the instruments of darkness'; and some editors believe that when Malcolm (at the end of Act IV) says that 'The Powers above/Put on their instruments' he is referring to their human instruments—Malcolm, Macduff and their soldiers.

The opposition between the good and evil supernatural is paralleled by similar contrasts between angel and devil, heaven and hell, truth and falsehood—and the opposites are frequently juxtaposed:

> This supernatural soliciting
> Cannot be ill; cannot be good.

> Merciful powers
> Restrain in me the cursed thoughts that nature
> Gives way to in repose!

> It is a knell
> That summons thee to heaven or to hell.

Several critics have pointed out the opposition in the play between night and day, life and death, grace and evil, a contrast which is reiterated more than four hundred times.[12]

The evidence for this has gone beyond imagery proper and most modern imagistic critics have extended their field to cover not merely metaphor and simile, but the visual symbols implied by the dialogue, which would be visible in performance, and even the iteration of key words. The Poet Laureate once remarked that *Macbeth* is about blood; and from the appearance of the bloody sergeant in the second scene of the play to the last scene of all, we have a continual vision of blood. Macbeth's sword in the battle 'smok'd with bloody execution'; he and Banquo seemed to 'bathe in reeking wounds'; the Sergeant's 'gashes cry for help'. The Second Witch comes from the bloody task of killing swine. The visionary dagger is stained with 'gouts of blood'. Macbeth, after the murder, declares that not all great Neptune's ocean will cleanse his hands:

> this my hand will rather
> The multitudinous seas incarnadine,
> Making the green one red.

Duncan is spoken of as the fountain of his sons' blood; his wounds

> look'd like a breach in nature
> For ruin's wasteful entrance.

70

The world had become a 'bloody stage'. Macbeth, before the murder of Banquo, invokes the 'bloody and invisible hand' of night. We are told of the twenty trenched gashes on Banquo's body and his ghost shakes his 'gory locks' at Macbeth, who is convinced that 'blood will have blood'. At the end of the banquet scene, he confesses wearily that he is 'stepp'd so far' in blood, that

> should I wade no more,
> Returning were as tedious as go o'er.

The Second Apparition, a bloody child, advises Macbeth to be 'bloody, bold, and resolute'. Malcolm declares that Scotland bleeds,

> and each new day a gash
> Is added to her wounds.

Lady Macbeth, sleep-walking, tries in vain to remove the 'damned spot' from her hands:

> Here's the smell of the blood still. All the perfumes of Arabia will not sweeten this little hand.

In the final scene, Macbeth's severed head is displayed on a pole. As Kott has recently reminded us, the subject of the play is murder, and the prevalence of blood ensures that we shall never forget the physical realities in metaphysical overtones.

Equally important is the iteration of sleep. The first statement of the theme is when the First Witch curses the Master of the *Tiger*:

> Sleep shall neither night nor day
> Hang upon his penthouse lid.

After the murder of Duncan, Macbeth and his wife

> sleep
> In the affliction of these terrible dreams
> That shake us nightly;

while Duncan, 'after life's fitful fever . . . sleeps well'. An anonymous lord looks forward to the overthrow of the tyrant, when they will be able to sleep in peace. Because of 'a great perturbation in nature', Lady Macbeth

> is troubled with thick coming fancies
> That keep her from her rest.

The key passage in the theme of sleeplessness, derived apparently from Holinshed and Seneca's *Hercules Furens*, occurs just after the murder of Duncan, when Macbeth hears a voice which cries 'Sleep no more!' It is really the echo of his own conscience. As Bradley noted, the voice 'denounced on him, as if his three names [Glamis, Cawdor, Macbeth] gave him three personalities to suffer in, the doom of sleeplessness'; and, as Murry puts it:

He has murdered Sleep, that is 'the death of each day's life'—that daily death of Time which makes Time human.

The murder of a sleeping guest, the murder of a sleeping king, the murder of a saintly old man, the murder, as it were, of sleep itself, carries with it the appropriate retribution of insomnia.[13]

As Murry's comment suggests, the theme of sleep is linked with that of time. Macbeth is

71

promised by the Weird Sisters that he will be king 'hereafter' and Banquo wonders if they 'can look into the seeds of time'. Macbeth, tempted by the thought of murder, declares that 'Present fears/Are less than horrible imaginings' and decides that 'Time and the hour runs through the roughest day'. Lady Macbeth says she feels 'The future in the instant'. In his soliloquy in the last scene of Act I, Macbeth speaks of himself as 'here upon this bank and shoal of time', time being contrasted with the sea of eternity. He pretends that he would not worry about the future, or about the life to come, if he could be sure of success in the present; and his wife implies that the conjunction of time and place for the murder will never recur. Just before the murder, Macbeth reminds himself of the exact time and place, so that he can relegate (as Stephen Spender suggests)[14] 'the moment to the past from which it will never escape into the future'. Macbeth is troubled by his inability to say amen, because he dimly realizes he has forfeited the possibility of blessing and because he knows that he has become 'the deed's creature'. The nightmares of the guilty pair and the return of Banquo from the grave symbolize the haunting of the present by the past. When Macbeth is informed of his wife's death, he describes how life has become for him a succession of meaningless days, the futility he has brought upon himself by his crimes:

> To-morrow, and to-morrow, and to-morrow,
> Creeps in this petty pace from day to day
> To the last syllable of recorded time,
> And all our yesterdays have lighted fools
> The way to dusty death.

At the very end of the play, Macduff announces that with the death of the tyrant 'The time is free' and Malcolm promises, without 'a large expense of time' to do what is necessary ('which would be planted newly with the time') and to bring back order from chaos 'in measure, time, and place'.

From one point of view *Macbeth* can be regarded as a play about the disruption of order through evil, and its final restoration.[15] The play begins with what the witches call a hurly-burly and ends with the restoration of order by Malcolm. Order is represented throughout by the bonds of loyalty; and chaos is represented by the powers of darkness with their upsetting of moral values ('Fair is foul and foul is fair'). The witches can raise winds to fight against the churches, to sink ships and destroy buildings: they are the enemies both of religion and of civilization. Lady Macbeth invokes the evil spirits to take possession of her; and, after the murder of Duncan, Macbeth's mind begins to dwell on universal destruction. He is willing to 'let the frame of things disjoint, both the worlds suffer' merely to be freed from his nightmares. Again, in his conjuration of the witches in the cauldron scene, he is prepared to risk absolute chaos, 'even till destruction sicken' through surfeit, rather than not obtain an answer. In his last days, Macbeth is 'aweary of the sun' and he wishes 'the estate of the world' were undone. Order in Scotland, even the moral order in the universe, can be restored only by his death. G. R. Elliott contrasts[16] the threefold hail with which Malcolm is greeted at the end of the play with the threefold hail of the witches on the blasted heath: they mark the destruction of order and its restoration.

All through the play ideas of order and chaos are juxtaposed. When Macbeth is first visited by temptation his 'single state of man' is shaken and 'nothing is but what is not'. In the next scene (I, iv) Shakespeare presents ideas of loyalty, duty, and the reward of faithful service, in contrast both to the treachery of the dead Thane of Cawdor and to the treacherous thoughts of the new thane. Lady Macbeth prays to be spared 'compunctious visitings of nature' and in the next scene, after the description of the 'pleasant seat' of the castle with its images of natural beauty, she expresses her gratitude and loyalty to the king. Before the murder, Macbeth reminds himself of the threefold tie of loyalty which binds him to Duncan, as kinsman, subject and host. He is afraid that the very stones will cry out against the unnaturalness of the murder, which is, in fact, accompanied by strange portents:

> Lamentings heard i' th' air, strange screams of death,
> And prophesying, with accents terrible,
> Of dire combustion and confus'd events
> New hatch'd to th' woeful time.

The frequent iteration of the word 'strange' is one of the ways by which Shakespeare underlines the disruption of the natural order.

Passages which older critics deplored, and which even H. N. Paul regarded[17] as flattery of King James, may be seen as part of the theme we have been discussing. Macbeth's curious discourse on dogs is one of these passages. It was inserted not mainly because of James's proclamation on the subject, but to stress the order of nature—*naturae benignitas*—'the diverse functions and variety within a single species testifying to an overruling harmony and design'; and it is used to persuade his tools to murder Banquo. In the scene in England, Malcolm's self-accusations —in particular his confession of wishing to uproar the universal peace and confound all unity on earth—are disorders contrasted with the virtues he pretends not to have and with the miraculous powers of the pious Edward.

Reference must be made to two other groups of images, which I have discussed elsewhere in some detail—those relating to equivocation and those which are concerned with the contrast between what the Porter calls desire and performance.[18] The theme of equivocation runs all through the play. It was suggested, no doubt, by the topicality of the subject at Father Garnet's trial, but this links up with 'the equivocation of the fiend/That lies like truth', the juggling fiends 'That keep the word of promise to our ear/And break it to our hope', and Macbeth's own equivocation after the murder of Duncan:

> Had I but died an hour before this chance,
> I had liv'd a blessed time; for, from this instant,
> There's nothing serious in mortality—
> All is but toys; renown and grace is dead;
> The wine of life is drawn, and the mere lees
> Is left this vault to brag of.

Macbeth's intention is to avert suspicion from himself by following his wife's advice to make their 'griefs and clamour roar upon' Duncan's death. But, as he speaks the words, the audience knows that he has unwittingly spoken the truth. Instead of lying like truth, he has told the truth while intending to deceive. As he expresses it later, when full realization has come to him, life has become meaningless, a succession of empty tomorrows, 'a tale told by an idiot'.

The gap between desire and performance, enunciated by the Porter, is expressed over and over again by Macbeth and his wife. It takes the form, most strikingly, in the numerous passages contrasting eye and hand, culminating in Macbeth's cry—

What hands are here? Ha! They pluck out mine eyes—

and in the scene before the murder of Banquo when the bloodstained hand is no longer Macbeth's, but Night's:

Come, seeling night,
Scarf up the tender eye of pitiful day,
And with thy bloody and invisible hand
Cancel and tear to pieces that great bond
Which keeps me pale.

In the sleep-walking scene, Lady Macbeth's unavailing efforts to wash the smell of the blood from her hand symbolize the indelibility of guilt; and Angus in the next scene declares that Macbeth feels

His secret murders sticking on his hands.

The soul is damned for the deeds committed by the hand.

It has recently been argued[19] that the opposition between the hand and eye provides the clearest explanation of that division in Macbeth between his clear 'perception of evil and his rapt drift into evil'. Lawrence W. Hyman suggests that Macbeth is able to do the murder only because of the deep division between his head and his hand. The

almost autonomous action of Macbeth's dagger, as if it had no connection with a human brain or a human heart, explains the peculiar mood that pervades the murder scene . . . As soon as he lays down the dagger, however, his 'eye' cannot help but see what the hand has done.

A study of the imagery and symbolism in Macbeth does not radically alter one's interpretation of the play. It would, indeed, be suspect if it did. In reading some modern criticisms of Shakespeare one has the feeling that the critic is reading between the lines and creating from the interstices a play rather different from the one which Shakespeare wrote and similar to a play the critic himself might have written. Such interpretations lead us away from Shakespeare; they drop a veil between us and the plays; and they substitute a formula for the living reality, a philosophy or a theology instead of a dramatic presentation of life. I have not attempted to reshape Macbeth to a particular ideological image, nor selected parts of the play to prove a thesis. Some selection had to be made for reasons of space, but I have tried to make the selection representative of the whole.

We must not imagine, of course, that Macbeth is merely an elaborate pattern of imagery. It is a play; and in the theatre we ought to recover, as best we may, a state of critical innocence. We should certainly not attempt to notice the images of clothing or breast-feeding or count the allusions to blood or sleep. But, just as Shakespeare conveys to us the unconscious minds of the characters by means of the imagery, so, in watching the play, we may be totally unconscious of the patterns of imagery and yet absorb them unconsciously by means of our imaginative response to the poetry. In this way they will be subsumed under the total experience of the play.

And what of the producer? It would be quite fatal for him to get his actors to underline the key images—to make them, as it were, italicize them with a knowing wink at the professors in the stalls or the students in the gallery. All we should ask of the producer in this matter is that he should give us what Shakespeare wrote, and all that Shakespeare wrote, and that he should not try to improve on the script provided by the dramatist.

© K. MUIR 1966

NOTES

1. C. F. E. Spurgeon, *Leading Motives in the Imagery of Shakespeare's Tragedies.*

2. K. Muir (ed.), *Macbeth* (1951), pp. xxxiii, 7.

3. H. L. Rogers has recently argued (*R.E.S.* 1965, p. 44) that the tailor may refer to a man associated in the public mind with the Garnet trial; as Father Garnet went under the name of 'Mr Farmer', equivocator, tailor and farmer were all allusions to the Gunpowder Plot and its aftermath.

4. *This Great Stage* (1948), *Magic in the Web* (1956).

5. *The Well Wrought Urn* (1947), pp. 22–49.

6. P. 17 above.

7. *The Royal Play of 'Macbeth'* (1950), p. 388.

8. *The Business of Criticism* (1959), p. 61. Cf. K. Muir, 'Shakespeare's Imagery—Then and Now', *Shakespeare Survey 18* (1965), p. 55.

9. K. Muir, *Macbeth*, p. lviii, and 'Shakespeare's Soliloquies', *Ocidente*, LXVII (1964), p. 65.

10. More questionably, Cleanth Brooks associates the babe images with the question, much debated in the play, of what constitutes manliness. See, especially, the discussion between Macbeth and his wife in I, vii and between Macbeth and the murderers in III, i. Macbeth, before he falls, declares:

> I dare do all that may become a man:
> Who dares do more is none.

He is humanized, it has been said, by his fears. When, at the end of the play, he can no longer feel fear, he dies like a hunted beast. This, in turn, links up with the animal imagery, which is of some importance in *Macbeth*, though less prevalent than in *King Lear* or *Othello*.

11. H. N. Paul, *op. cit.* p. 391.

12. F. C. Kolbe, *Shakespeare's Way* (1930), pp. 21–2, Cf. also G. Wilson Knight, *The Imperial Theme* (1931) L. C. Knights, *Explorations* (1946), Roy Walker, *The Time is Free* (1949).

13. Cf. J. M. Murry, *Shakespeare* (1935), p. 333.

14. *Penguin New Writing*, no. 3, pp. 115–26. I am indebted to this article for several points in this paragraph.

15. Cf. Robert Speaight, *Nature in Shakespearian Tragedy* (1955), L. C. Knights, *op. cit.* and G. Wilson Knight, *op. cit.*

16. *Dramatic Providence in Macbeth* (1958), p. 228.

17. *Op. cit.* pp. 367 ff., 392 ff., 359 ff.

18. *Macbeth*, pp. xxvii–xxxii.

19. Lawrence W. Hyman, *Tennessee Studies* (1960), pp. 97–100.

AN APPROACH TO
SHAKESPEARIAN TRAGEDY:
THE 'ACTOR' IMAGE IN *MACBETH*

BY

V. Y. KANTAK

I

If Shakespeare continues to appeal in the modern world it is because of his peculiar 'independence', independence of any intellectual creed, moral or other, which might gain acceptance in one age and lose its plausibility in another. In an important sense, Shakespeare is independent of his time: he does, indeed, express his age perfectly; 'but he expresses it a little too perfectly to be its child'. And the time he expressed was marked by the intense vitality of the Elizabethans, by their confident and adventurous participation in a world of expanding horizons. It was a time of deep and rapid change, and Shakespeare asserts the significant human values during a period which produced a kind of fusion of Renaissance action with medieval thought. We are still moved by the momentum then generated. Even the Orient, lately awakened and still rubbing her eyes after a night of bad dreams, now feels its pressure. We are again living in a time of deep and rapid change, torn between man's self-sufficiency and the need to have faith in a power beyond him. In such a time as ours Shakespeare's steadily human values make special appeal, the more so because the confidence of the earlier day has been replaced by uncertainty, challenge and peril.

The integrity of Shakespeare's vision is, of course, something which cannot be expressed within any single, simple formula; on the other hand we may say with assurance that, whatever its complexity and depth, it owes its strength to a complete response to the wholeness of creation. His is a 'round' vision which sees all sides at once and as one—a quality which is painfully bewildering to rigid minds. He knows all men with that sympathy which each feels for himself. His art is organic through and through; we get little feeling of artifice or mechanical contrivance; it seems to be art strangely congruent with Nature. And again and again when he treats of essential tragic evil no less than when he treats of the humour of a Falstaff or the sunshine fun and 'the deep marriage-consciousness' of his ladies, he confronts us with a peerless wisdom.

Generations of critics have tried, often vainly, to explain and expound this integrity that is Shakespeare's. The effort to interpret it must necessarily go on; but one thing has to be stressed—any interpretation that loses sight of the essential element in his appeal does more harm than good. And, remembering this truth, we are bound to believe that certain currents in the ever-increasing stream of modern Shakespearian criticism are inclined to bear us away from the essential core of his appeal. The recent concentration upon the nature and function of poetic imagery has, it is true, made us aware of a new dimension—the power exerted by these images in weaving a fabric full of imaginative significance. At the same time, we are forced to recognize that, in the excessive zeal with which these explorations have been pursued, there is developing a dangerous separation between the poetry and the drama, with the result that the uniqueness of Shakespeare's works is being obscured.

In view of this, two propositions may be submitted: (1) The 'character' approach, obviously erroneous in the form it took during the nineteenth century, is still a legitimate approach basically related to the dramatic form. In attending to the imagery we should not overlook its importance. (2) The poetry that a character speaks, in an important sense, 'belongs' to and is revelatory of that character. It cannot simply be regarded as though it 'belonged' only to Shakespeare in the way lyric poetry belongs to an author.

The recent emphasis on imagery and the symbolic element started as a reaction to the excesses of the nineteenth-century concentration upon Shakespeare's characters. It was indeed proper that the cruder and more naïve manifestations of that vogue should have been held up to ridicule. The treatment of Shakespearian characters as if they were living human beings who had some-how made their escape from their literary situations could lead only to curious, and sometimes comic, biographical probings which, although sometimes innocuous (as in the question, 'How did the boy in *Henry V* learn to speak French?'), were often of a kind fully deserving L. C Knights' slashing judgement: 'The habit of regarding Shakespeare's persons as "friends for life" or may be "deceased acquaintances" is responsible for most of the vagaries that serve as criticism.'[1] Naturally, the attack on this 'character' approach centred upon Bradley, whose monumental work represents the best in that earlier tradition which Coleridge may be said to have initiated. For Knights, Bradley's attitude seems more that of a detective than of a critic, and he takes exception to the pronouncement which provides the basis for all Bradley's investigations: 'The centre of the tragedy may be said with equal truth to lie in action issuing from character, or in character issuing in action... what we feel strongly, as a tragedy advances to its close, is that the calamities and catastrophe follow inevitably from the deeds of men, and that the main source of these deeds is character.[2]

It may, of course, readily be admitted that Bradley tends to treat Shakespearian characters as living human beings, seeking to interpret their words, their motives, their activities in terms we normally assume to be true of the world of living persons, whereas these characters exist only within the carefully determined shadow-world which is the drama in which they make their appearances. They have no reality other than that which is fixed by the words given to them by Shakespeare. Bradley himself was aware of the dangers involved in straying too far from the play's words, but he insisted that the response in the mind of reader or spectator was funda-mentally important: 'Any answer to the question proposed ought to correspond with, or to represent in terms of the understanding, our imaginative and emotional experience in reading the tragedies. We have, of course, to do our best by study and effort to make this experience true to Shakespeare; but that done, the experience is the matter to be interpreted.'[3] In other words, how else can we interpret the characters and what they feel and how they act except by using our understanding of people's motives and behaviour in our ordinary lives? The ability to read the clues provided in the dialogue of the dramas is basically the same as the ability we bring to bear upon our understanding of living persons around us. 'Action issuing from character or character issuing in action' is the basic element in drama; it is what initially determines the kind of total response we make to it as a work of art.

Exploring character in action, Bradley came to the conclusion that the ultimate power in

Shakespeare's tragic world cannot be adequately described as a law or an order which is just or benevolent, nor can it be described as a fate whether malicious or merely indifferent to human happiness or goodness; there is in it an equal emphasis, a sort of a tension, between the destiny within and the destiny without. 'Shakespeare', said Bradley, 'was not attempting to justify the ways of God to men. He was writing tragedy, and tragedy would not be tragedy if it were not a painful mystery.'[4] What is central in that view is that Shakespeare maintains a kind of even balance of vision, holding in check our natural desire to embrace some religious or philosophical conception that would explain all. This view is now being assailed with the shift of attention to the symbolic force of imagery. Critics are now trying to show, for instance, that in the total poetical design of *Macbeth* there is an assertion of a moral order and a complete acceptance of the Christian ethic. It is argued that Shakespeare is closer to medieval traditions than was hitherto supposed, and *Macbeth* is now being read simply as a 'Morality' in which the characters figure as symbols of moral entities all diagrammatically disposed to illustrate the Christian code. Macbeth, the evil man who makes the fatal choice, is poised between Lady Macbeth and Banquo, the bad and the good angels respectively.

Irving Ribner thus believes that 'as Shakespeare became more and more absorbed in the religious and ethical dimensions of tragedy he concentrated more and more on the development of the symbol with *a corollary unconcern for character consistency*'.[5] He would thus explain Bradley's failure to see a moral order in Shakespeare's tragedies: 'stage characters analysed as though they were human beings could reflect only the mystery and seeming indirection of human life. Bradley could lead his readers only to a Shakespeare without positive belief, to a conception of tragedy merely as a posing of unanswerable questions, and to a moral system in the plays which is upon close analysis not moral at all'.[6] Such an approach, however, seems to ignore the fact that 'the posing of unanswerable questions' is, in the end, the very foundation of tragedy. The peculiar tension in a tragedy arises from our difficulty in accepting, not from our reluctance to accept the moral order. The moral order is there, but something has to run counter to it to produce that tension. Bradley found that force centred in the character itself, for instance, in Macbeth as he lives through the ravages of evil. It would seem that the symbolic pattern and all the thematic imagery of the play have to be brought into contact with that element to produce the tragic effect peculiar to the Shakespearian conception. Even the witches have significance only as an opportunity for evil without to respond to evil within.

There is surely something wrong in the approach that considers Shakespeare's realism of character as a sort of technical proficiency valuable in its way but not at all very essential to his tragic vision. It is true that the characters are not 'real', but part of Shakespeare's artistry lies in convincing us that they are and in getting us emotionally involved with them. The symbolic function they seem to perform in the over-all pattern of the play does not exist independently. We have to create it in our minds by entering fully into the real lifelike situation of character and action. It is only thus that the tragedy has the effect of creating 'a kind of tension beween feeling and action, between our emotional involvement in a specific situation and our rational contemplation of its meaning'. It is precisely this kind of tension that is centred in the character of Macbeth. The 'over-all intellectual concerns of the play' require Macbeth to be an unredeemable sinner but his poetic ability, his power to grasp fully and concretely what is happening to himself, sets up disturbance in our minds and makes his thematically ordained damnation so painful to accept.

This effect Bradley would put down simply to the fact that Macbeth happens to have the poet's imagination; but the new critics find it difficult to accept that statement, because they feel that such a reading of Macbeth's character implies confusion between life and art. Kenneth Muir, commenting on Macbeth's soliloquy in I, vii, says, 'The imagery of the speech shows that Macbeth is haunted by the horror of the deed, and impresses that horror on the audience. But if we go further and pretend that this poetic imagery is a proof that Macbeth had a powerful imagination, that he was, in fact, a poet, we are confusing real life with drama.'[7] In other words, the poetry that a character speaks is not to be considered in relation to and as revelatory of his nature, but only as part of the general poetic design of the play. What we must ask is whether this is not confusing drama with what it is not. Surely a closer approach to the truth rests in H. S. Wilson's judgement:

We may think that the 'confusion' of Macbeth's poetry with Shakespeare's is precisely the effect Shakespeare aimed at in the theatre. As we listen to Macbeth's eloquence, we forget about Shakespeare the poet, we forget that we are listening to a poem, we think only of the figure imaginatively evoked for us and embodied upon the stage....If this is to confuse drama with real life, it is also the 'Willing suspension of disbelief that constitutes poetic faith'....We feel that Macbeth is a poetic person and we value him for the poetry of his utterance.[8]

Macbeth's poetry has, in fact, the effect of confounding those who seek to read in the play the most perfect illustration of the Christian theme of sin and damnation; it is no less an inconvenience to those others who arrive at the same conclusion from an exclusive attention to the poetic pattern created by the imagery regardless of who uses the images and at what point of the action. By giving Macbeth poetic power Shakespeare has achieved for us most poignantly the ambivalence of the tragic effect that Aristotle described. That ambivalent response is inescapable if we honestly confront the 'principle of morality' which is present in Macbeth's imaginative fears and which enables him to grasp fully the moral implications of his action, to participate in the full horror of it and to report the havoc caused by the evil within him. Any criticism that fails to see the impressiveness of Macbeth in his final self-portrayal of his soliloquy, 'To-morrow and to-morrow...' seems surely to miss whatever tragic purpose Shakespeare had in mind. Logically it should be the last stage of the corruption caused by evil; and yet somehow, as Santayana said, 'Macbeth is divinely human here!' Abercrombie is right in asserting that the final harmony of good and evil is achieved in the character of Macbeth which creates and endures evil. Macbeth has staked everything and lost and for nothing—a bleak imbecile futility: 'But he seizes on the appalling moment and masters even this; he masters it by knowing it absolutely and completely by forcing even this quintessence of all evil to live before him with the zest and terrible splendour of his own unquenchable mind.'[9]

Kenneth Muir comments on this, 'The fallacy here is simply that Abercrombie is confusing the powers of expression possessed by Macbeth with the poetic powers of Shakespeare himself. Once again it must be emphasized that because Shakespeare makes Macbeth talk as only a great poet could talk, we are not to assume that Macbeth is a great poet: he is merely part of a great poem.'[10] One might have great difficulty in understanding what, according to Kenneth Muir, belongs to Macbeth as a component of the play and what to Shakespeare. Of course, all, in one sense, is Shakespeare's poetry, but within that larger ambit there is the simulated life of a man who is given his *own speech* and his *own activity*.

It is easy to see how far this kind of criticism wrests the poetry from its dramatic moorings. For Muir, 'Every character in a poetic play may speak poetry; but this poetry does not necessarily reflect their poetic dispositions—it is merely a medium. The bloody Sergeant utters bombastic language, not because he is himself bombastic, but because such language was considered appropriate to epic narration.... So too with Macbeth, we may say his imagery expresses his unconscious mind...but we must not say he is therefore a poet.'[11] The important point missed here is that Macbeth's words are distinct in kind from those of the bombastic Sergeant; Macbeth's speech alone has the power of suggesting the subconscious—and, after all, whose subconscious does his lines express if not that of himself?

II

It looks as though we are still far from arriving at a balanced approach to the functioning of the images of a Shakespeare play despite the numerous studies accomplished in this field. Few, indeed, are inquiries of the kind suggested in Clemen's *The Development of Shakespeare's Imagery* and Morozov's *The Individualization of Shakespeare's Characters through Imagery*, in which attempts are made to relate the function of imagery to the development of character. A statement such as 'Every character in a poetic play may speak poetry but that does not necessarily reflect their poetic dispositions' leaves unexplained how it is that, though all speak poetry, the poetic speech of one has a distinct quality setting it off from that of another. There is consistency in the speech of a character; each is given a sort of personal idiom which is maintained throughout. When there is a pronounced change or growth in the character it is reflected in a corresponding change of tone and imagery and in the rhythm of the poetic speech. Thus, for example, there is such a change in Romeo when he learns to face the dangers of his situation and emerges into maturity. When we see him in Mantua at the beginning of Act v we at once perceive by his first words that he is a new man entirely.

Imagery, too, is used to intensify some peculiar aspect of the developing action as in the celebrated case of the commerce between Iago and Othello in which Othello is found using Iago's imagery unconsciously as Iago's plan has begun to succeed. If we neglect the principle of character individualization implicit·in the imagery of Shakespeare's poetic medium we should be obscuring the effect of a potent dramatic device he uses again and again. The variety that he rings on that medium is disposed in relation to character and developing action. It is necessary to assume that the imagery does two things at once; it illustrates the theme and expresses character. Often the speaker may be unconscious of the full force of his words, as Banquo is unconscious of the deeper significance of his references to 'the temple-haunting martlet' and the genial quality of the air at Inverness castle. His words advance the theme of the grace of bounteous Nature and are heavy with the anticipatory irony of the hospitable castle presently turning into a charnel-house. But at the same time they embody his own character as that of one who, though not far above common humanity, can yet say truthfully, 'In the great hand of God I stand'. But whether conscious or unconscious, the personal reference is never entirely lost and the poetry is never reduced to a purely *choral* comment on the character or the action. The image is at once a reflection of the speaker's state of mind and a poetic vehicle for developing and enriching the play's thematic content.

It is necessary to stress this double value, since the increasing study of imagery has induced many critics to view the images from one point of view merely; and this has led to a regarding of the characters, not as having the consistency and functional unity of living beings, but only as more or less abstract counters which serve as vehicles for Shakespeare's poetry. Charlton's complaint against those critics who treat Shakespeare's characters as 'plastic symbols in an arabesque of esoteric imagery' seems to be justified. The result is that character, event, action and the motives behind the action, all lose the normal sense we attach to them, leaving with us a continuous dramatic poem—in reality, more like a lyric—which only because of certain extraneous features we call drama. This argues a fundamental misconception about the category 'drama'. Is it possible to talk about that category without assuming that a simulation of the kind of unity of motive and behaviour that characterize the actions of living human beings is essential to it? What may be called 'the fundamental realism' of drama, not the stylistic development called 'realistic' drama, requires that everything in a play, even a poetic play, be cast in the shape of human activity making it an image of men in action. The poetic pattern aids the plausibility of that image. It is itself made up of the words uttered by characters and its logic is the logic of men expressing themselves in free activity. That is what makes the distinction between 'dramatic poem' and 'poetic drama' not merely fanciful but real.

Drama is an art which eventuates in words but which in its essence 'is at once more primitive, more subtle and more direct than either word or concept'—that is the irreducible idea of drama, says Francis Fergusson, and in the following words he merely reiterates what has always been a fundamental premise of dramatic criticism:

But a drama, as distinguished from the lyric is not primarily a composition in the verbal medium; the words result, as one might put it, from the underlying structure of incident and character.... *The process of becoming acquainted with a play is like that of becoming acquainted with a person*; it is an empirical and inductive process.... We seek to grasp the quality of a man's life, by an imaginative effort, through his appearances, his words, and his deeds.... We grasp the stage-life of a play through the plot, characters and the words which manifest it.[12]

Criticism in which this element of simulated human activity becomes something merely adventitious misses the force of the poetry as well. What distinguishes tragedy is its 'activist' character, making man 'the arbiter of his own values'. In Shakespearian drama the springs of action are volitional and arise directly out of the Elizabethan pre-occupation with the problem of moral responsibility, 'which is seen at its simplest in *Doctor Faustus*, and its most complex in *Hamlet* and at its most naïve in, say, *The White Devil*'.[13]

Wilson Knight has exhorted us to take a Shakespeare play as an *expanding* metaphor. 'Though the original vision has been projected into forms roughly correspondent with actuality', he said, 'the persons ultimately, are not human at all, but purely symbols of a poetic vision'.[14] 'To analyse the sequence of events, the "cause" linking dramatic motive to action and of action to result in time, is a blunder instinctive to the human intellect.'[15] L. C. Knights has maintained that in a poetic play our 'apprehension of the whole can be obtained by a lively attention to the parts whether they have an immediate bearing on the main action or "illustrate" character or not'.[16] And more recently, D. A. Traversi has declared that Shakespeare's use of symbolism from *Macbeth* onwards implies a new conception of plot, without giving us an indication as to what that new conception is. All these pronouncements have a bearing on the progression within a play. The normal way of understanding that progression as the linking of dramatic motive to action and of action to result in time, far from being a blunder, is what distinguishes a poetic drama like *Macbeth* from a dramatic poem like *The Waste Land*. The images in *Macbeth* have their peculiar force because of the situation they are uttered in, the person who utters them and the stage of his dramatic mental history at which he utters them. The images of *The Waste Land* follow a different kind of progression, and not being linked with the line of development that drama requires, can look back and forward more freely, all drawn, as it were, by a centripetal force to the dominant mood and vision of the poem. All the 'dramatic matter' of the poem whether ritualistic, situational or of character (Madam Sosostris and the Tarot pack, Tiresias, the typist girl and the carbuncular young man, Cleopatra-Elizabeth on the barge, Hieronymo, Phlebas the Phoenician, Mr Eugenides the Smyrna merchant, Stetson or the more shrouded figures like those of the Fisher King, Buddha-St Augustine or Christ), is held together by another logic than the progression implied in drama and responds to the over-all control of an impulse which is primarily lyrical. Whereas all that happens in a Shakespeare play is subjected to the gradual unfolding of a vision through the imaging of a volitional activity of characters issuing in action. The images aid and illuminate that process; they strengthen the total pattern, making the relation between character and action more intense.

By concentrating attention on poetic imagery in isolation from this progression, numerous modern critics, on the one hand, over-simplify and blur the actual complexity of a poetic play and, on the other, encourage an extremely subjective approach which is indefensible. T. R. Henn pertinently asks: 'Does the plot now become merely a frame-work for the dramatic poetry, or rather for a particular aspect of that "poetic content"? Are the ethical problems, the roots of will and choice in character, merged in a larger unity to which we are given no clue save our total "poetic response" to the play? And if that is so, are we committed to a new subjective aestheticism in which the image becomes paramount; even though it is, in essence as in fact, a device for communicating intense passion in speech?'[17] Even T. S. Eliot had only asked that we read character and plot in the understanding of the 'subterrene music' of the play. But the latter-day critics have gone farther; they have brought that music above ground, one fears, by simultaneously depressing the foreground of character and action out of sight, reversing the normal approach. The effect is not perhaps unlike judging a photographic portrait by looking at the negative.

III

Perhaps it is possible to show how an image can simultaneously reinforce both theme and character-in-action by examining a notable passage like Macbeth's last major soliloquy:

> Tomorrow, and to-morrow, and to-morrow,
> Creeps in this petty pace from day to day
> To the last syllable of recorded time,
> And all our yesterdays have lighted fools
> The way to dusty death. Out, out, brief candle!

82

Life's but a walking shadow, a poor player
That struts and frets his hour upon the stage
And then is heard no more: it is a tale
Told by an idiot, full of sound and fury,
Signifying nothing.

It has been remarked how several lines of imagery previously apprehended seem to converge and reach here a kind of summation—the mechanical procession of Time infructuous, contrasted with all the earlier emphasis on child images; the opposition of darkness and light, muffled sunlight and starlight, the fire below the Witches' cauldron and the light of the domestic candle lighting the way to bed (a fling back to the weird shadows made by Lady Macbeth's sleepwalking); the empty posturing of the stage-actor and finally the reverberation of sound echoing. But the image that powerfully stands out in the whole series is that of the 'poor player'. A little pondering reveals its peculiar appositeness to what happens in the play as a whole as well as to Macbeth's character and destiny. It is in fact the dominant master-conception 'underlying this varied but inter-locked imagery of desire and act, outward appearance and inward purpose, the clothes that fit another and thus cannot be borrowed, time and the moment of timelessness, the pattern we would impose on time and time's freedom from our contriving'.[18]

What is its implication for Macbeth's character? The closing phrase of 'the statement of evil' presents something like the transformation and the cutting adrift of man from the firm nexus that binds him to Nature into the world of things and manoeuvrable illusions. Perhaps the marionette is the closest objectification of that effect. He ceases to be a free agent and becomes completely determined. Time no longer confers freedom, but binds, is barren. Macbeth has lost Time the renewer and has come into the grip of Time who binds him to his past. Nature combines, fosters mutuality and breaks through into the future with the possibility of further freedom, holding the door open. In its place there is now the mere mechanical joinery of the puppet which mocks the unity implicit in Nature.

This is connected with Macbeth's isolation which, signalled by Lady Macbeth's anxious query, 'How now, my lord, why do you keep alone?', grows into an enormous exclusion from all that is natural. Insensibility to natural feeling ('She should have died here-after!') becomes an impenetrable wall separating him from his kind. There is only one thing that remains before Macbeth is utterly simplified and placed for ever in past time, and that is the power of the actor to see himself as performing. Before *his* light is finally extinguished this 'stage-light' must afford him one glimpse of himself in the stage posture of the walking shadow whose empty sound and fury is presently going to be no more. Thenceforward, it is the mask that animates the person with the animation peculiar to stage-types. The sounding of alarums and Macbeth's hollow, nervous brag herald the end. It is in the world of melodrama that Macbeth dies and the melodramatic necessity of 'Behold, where stands the usurper's cursed head' must be satisfied. But we know better and refrain from judgement.

It is easy to see how this image of the stage-actor gives unity to all the various strands of meaning conveyed by the play's imagery. L. C. Knights emphasized the numerous images that signify the great bond of Nature which makes the whole world kin and which Macbeth tears to pieces. All these images are made to stand in sharp contrast with the automation of the stage-actor into which Macbeth is propelled irresistibly as he cuts himself off from the vital connection.

Cleanth Brooks, brilliantly analysing the garment imagery, brings out the symbolic force of the 'naked babe and the manly cloak'.[19] Borrowed robes that are ill-fitting, painted faces, daggers 'unmannerly breeched with gore' have all a reference, however dim, to the mechanics of theatrical action. Similarly, as Kenneth Muir notices, the meaningful opposition between the hand and the eye or the heart, between the eye and the other senses, has a relation to the business of the stage. Macbeth's great concern is to divorce the hand from the heart. He observes the functioning of his own organs with a strange objectivity, much as does the actor upon the stage. In the same way, reiteration of images emphasizing time free and time controlled, living light and light smothered, desire and act, inward purpose and outward appearance has a scarce-hidden reference to the movement from life to the illusion of the stage.

The different stages of Macbeth's entire career seem to reflect that movement. Before the evil has gained firm lodgment his references to this element are marked by questioning, not acceptance: 'Why do you dress me in borrow'd robes?' When he is busy in Nature's mischief his one wish is to 'disconnect': 'Let the eye wink at the hand,' and the heart not recognize what the hand is doing. Macbeth's wish seems to be to do the act as if it is a stage affair, for to engage his heart would mean disaster. In the subsequent scenes his prayer is ironically fulfilled; the illusion is confirmed into the only reality for him. The things in his head can be acted before they are 'scanned' till 'the very firstlings' of his heart become the firstlings of his hand. He is no more conscious of the opposition between the hand and the heart; what he had been 'acting' has now become confirmed in nature. His last sin against humanity, the murder of Lady Macduff and her children, is undertaken with a perfect spontaneity indicating the progress in the 'disconnection'.

Macbeth's very first full encounter with the idea of the murder that would lead him to the 'golden round' is cast in theatrical terms:

> Two truths are told,
> As happy prologues to the swelling act
> Of the imperial theme.

'This is the birth of evil in Macbeth. He might have had ambitious thoughts before, may even have intended the murder but now for the first time he feels its oncoming reality' (Wilson Knight). Macbeth's words at this critical moment echo the 'wooden O' passage in *Henry V*:

> A kingdom for a stage, princes to act,
> And monarchs to behold the swelling scene.

'Prologue', 'swelling', 'act' and 'the imperial theme' are all there. The Chorus in *Henry V* is calling attention to the deficiencies of the theatre, 'prologue-like' begging the audience to eke out those deficiencies with their own imagination—a strictly theatrical business, word and thing. And Macbeth himself at the first onset begins to enact his role in his imagination though the horrid image unfixes his hair and makes his seated heart knock at his ribs against the use of nature. In fact the whole passage is strangely filled with suggestions of the stage:

> My thought, whose murder yet is but fantastical,
> Shakes so my single state of man that function
> Is smother'd in surmise, and nothing is
> But what is not.

Macbeth is rapt and saying to himself, 'Of things now about me I have no perception, being intent wholly on that which has no existence' (Johnson). Nor does it seem an accident that stage imagery should come to the fore again when Lady Macbeth dwells upon the same event in her apostrophe to the 'murth'ring ministers':

> Come, thick night,
> And pall thee in the dunnest smoke of hell,
> That my keen knife see not the wound it makes,
> Nor heaven peep through the blanket of the dark,
> To cry, 'Hold, hold!'

'Hell', 'pall', 'knife', 'dark'—'The peculiar and appropriate dress for Tragedy is a *pall* and a *knife*. When Tragedies were represented, the stage was hung with black' (Clarendon), and it has been suggested that the 'heaven' or canopy over the stage likewise underwent some gloomy transformation. Even 'the blanket of the dark' might have some relation to the sable hangings.

When the act is performing, just before and after it, images contrasting appearance with reality multiply, and suggestions of theatrical illusion keep seeping through with varying nuances of significance. Macbeth sees 'the dagger of the mind, a false creation' and rubs his eyes with 'Mine eyes are made the fools o'th'other senses'. Lady Macbeth attempts to allay his fears after the deed with ''Tis the eye of childhood that fears the painted devil', and puns horribly about gilding the grooms' faces to make it seem their guilt. There is the grim play-acting of the Hell-gate Porter. There is Macduff's wild adjuration, 'Shake off this downy sleep, death's counterfeit...and see the great doom's image!' And through all the tumult we hear the agonized native voice of Macbeth attempting, as it were, a disconnection between his natural self and his 'stage' self who has performed the deed. 'To know my deed, 'twere best not to know myself.' And there is at least one appalling instance of play-acting on the part of Macbeth in which the hypocrite, the deceiver, merges into the 'hypocrite', the actor. When the murder is discovered Macbeth utters words which are meant to deceive but which curiously at the same time express his deepest feelings:

> Had I but died an hour before this chance,
> I had liv'd a blessed time; for, from this instant,
> There's nothing serious in mortality;
> All is but toys: renown and grace is dead;
> The wine of life is drawn, and the mere lees
> Is left this vault to brag of.

'Macbeth intends', says Murry, 'the monstrous hypocrisy of a conventional lament for Duncan; but as the words leave his lips they change their nature and become a doom upon himself.'[20] (These lines recall his 'real' lament in the later soliloquies—'I have lived long enough; my way of life has fall'n into the sere, the yellow leaf...'. It is a curious effect for which there is no parallel, and with it Macbeth seems to have entered fully into the theatrical image of himself. Here the face and mask are one.)

It is thus that in his last moment of deep sentience the image of the stage actor comes to his mind as the fitting symbol of what he has become. It not merely illustrates the theme but expresses character, for it arises from Macbeth's poetic power and his radiant self-knowledge to the last. What is more, it gives a certain direction to our response to the whole tragic spectacle. The governing master-conception has the effect of keeping the play's meaning and whatever ethic it implied well within the confines of the naturalistic ethic of Shakespearian tragedy. It is important that Macbeth's growth should be symbolized by the image of the actor, but what is still more important is that he should be able to see himself as one. The final verdict on him is not what is conveyed by the word 'damnation' nor by the word 'redemption'. *Macbeth* is placed in an ethic which is 'open' not closed. 'While we must recognize the firm orientation of "good" and "evil" we do not identify with one and contemplate the other either openly or secretly. Macbeth's nature unfolds itself, and is unfolded for us. This enactment is entirely self-supporting; it requires no moral props, no philosophical buttressing.'[21]

NOTES

1. L. C. Knights, *Explorations* (1946), p. 16.
2. A. C. Bradley, *Shakespearian Tragedy*.
3. *Ibid.*
4. *Ibid.*
5. Irving Ribner, *Patterns in Shakespearian Tragedy* (1960), p. 3. [Italics mine.]
6. *Ibid.*
7. Kenneth Muir, *Macbeth* (Arden Shakespeare), 1951, p. lix.
8. Harold S. Wilson, *On the Design of Shakespearian Tragedy* (1957), p. 69.
9. L. Abercrombie, *The Idea of Great Poetry* (1925), p. 176.
10. Muir, *op. cit.* p. ix.
11. *Ibid.* p. lix.
12. Francis Fergusson, *The Idea of a Theatre* (1949), pp. 24–5. [Italics mine.]
13. T. R. Henn, *The Harvest of Tragedy* (1956), p. 152.
14. G. Wilson Knight, *The Wheel of Fire* (1930).
15. G. Wilson Knight, *The Imperial Theme* (1931).
16. Knights, *op. cit.* p. 18.
17. Henn, *op. cit.* p. 153.
18. John Lawlor, *The Tragic Sense in Shakespeare* (1960), p. 130.
19. Cleanth Brooks, *The Well Wrought Urn* (1947), *passim.*
20. J. Middleton Murry, *Shakespeare* (1936), p. 332.
21. Graham Martin, *Interpretations*, edited by John Wain (1955), p. 30.